British English

Personal Best

A1 Beginner

Student's Book and **Workbook** combined edition

B

Series Editor
Jim Scrivener

Student's Book Author
Graham Fruen

Workbook Author
Daniel Barber

Richmond

Language App, unit-by-unit grammar and vocabulary games

Writing practice p67

Places

LANGUAGE   *there is/are* ■ places in a town

6A   City or village?

1   Match the words in the box with places 1–6.

| bank   bus stop   restaurant
hotel   supermarket   post office |

1 _____   3 _____   5 _____
2 _____   4 _____   6 _____

Personal Best

Go to Vocabulary practice: places in a town, page 120

2   **A**   Look at the pictures of Whycocomagh in Canada. Is it a city, town or village?

B   Read the text and tick (✔) the things Whycocomagh has.

1 shopping centre ☐   3 cinema ☐   5 school ☐
2 supermarket ☐   4 nightclub ☐   6 restaurants ☐

An unusual job offer

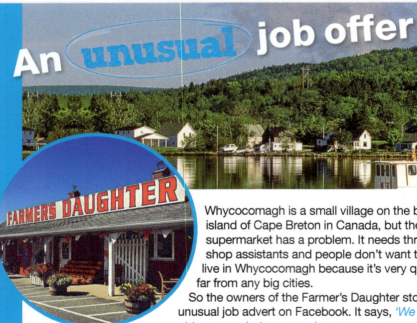

Whycocomagh is a small village on the beautiful island of Cape Breton in Canada, but the local supermarket has a problem. It needs three new shop assistants and people don't want to come to live in Whycocomagh because it's very quiet and far from any big cities.

So the owners of the Farmer's Daughter store put an unusual job advert on Facebook. It says, *'We can't give you big money, but we can give you an awesome life'* … and they offer over 8 km² of free land!

Thousands of people from around the world are interested and want to work in the village, so now the supermarket has some new shop assistants. But what's the village really like? We talk to Kelly Jenkins, a teacher at the village school.

Tell us about Whycocomagh, Kelly.
It's small, but it's beautiful. There's a school, a post office and the local supermarket, of course! There are also some hotels and restaurants for tourists.

Is there a shopping centre or a cinema?
No, there isn't! There aren't any big shops and there isn't a cinema or a nightclub. But there are some wonderful people here. Everyone is very friendly.

Are there any problems?
Yes, there are … but life's boring without any problems!

3   Complete the sentences with the words in the box. Check your answers in the text.

| isn't   's   aren't   are (x2)   is |

1 There _____ a school.
2 _____ there a shopping centre?
3 There _____ any big shops.

4 There _____ a cinema.
5 There _____ some wonderful people.
6 _____ there any problems?

4 Look at the sentences in exercise 3 again and choose the correct options to complete the rules. Then read the Grammar box.

1 We use *there's* and *there isn't* with *singular* / *plural* nouns.
2 We use *there are* and *there aren't* with *singular* / *plural* nouns.
3 We use *some* / *any* with plural nouns in positive sentences.
4 We use *some* / *any* with plural nouns in negative sentences and questions.

📖 **Grammar**	*there is/are*		
Positive:	**Negative:**	**Questions:**	**Short answers:**
There's a cinema.	**There isn't** a museum.	**Is there** a park?	Yes, **there is**. No, **there isn't**.
There are some shops.	**There aren't** any cafés.	**Are there** any hotels?	Yes, **there are**. No, **there aren't**.

Go to Grammar practice: *there is/are, page 101*

5 In pairs, say if you want to live in Whycocomagh. Explain your answers.

I don't want to live in Wycocomagh because there …

6 ▶6.3 Complete the text with the correct form of *there is/are*. Listen and check.

This is the beautiful city of Lavasa in India. ¹_____ some nice flats near the river. ²_____ a post office, a police station and ³_____ some great restaurants and cafés. ⁴_____ a train station, but if you need to travel by train, you can take a taxi to Pune, which is 60 km away. However, ⁵_____ something strange about Lavasa … nobody lives here! ⁶_____ any people in the flats. At the weekends, ⁷_____ some tourists in the restaurants and hotels, but they're on holiday.

7 A ▶6.4 **Pronunciation:** linking consonants and vowels Listen and repeat the sentences from exercise 6. Pay attention to how the sounds link together.

1 There's‿a post‿office.
2 There‿isn't‿a train station.
3 There‿aren't‿any people.
4 There‿are some tourists.

B ▶6.5 Say the sentences linking the sounds together. Listen, check and repeat.

1 There's‿a hospital.
2 Is there‿a bank?
3 There‿are some‿offices.
4 There‿aren't‿any museums.
5 There‿isn't‿a park.
6 Are there‿any schools?

Go to Communication practice: Student A page 138, Student B page 146

8 A ▶6.6 Listen to the conversation. Where does Erica live? Is she happy there?

B ▶6.6 Are the sentences about the area where Erica lives true (T) or false (F)? Listen again and check.

1 There's a big park. _____
2 There's a supermarket. _____
3 There aren't any shops. _____
4 There's a café in her street. _____
5 There isn't a bus stop near her house. _____
6 There are some good restaurants. _____

9 Ask and answer the questions in pairs.

Where do you live?
Is it a city, a town or a village?
What's your area like?
Is there a …?
Are there any …?

Personal Best Write about a city, town or village you know well.

6B City art

1 **A** Look at the pictures of public art on page 53. Do you like them? Why/Why not?

B Read the text quickly. In which cities can you see the three pieces of art?

> 🔧 **Skill** **reading in detail**
>
> **We sometimes have to read part of a text in detail to understand it well.**
> - Read the question and find the paragraph of the text that has the information you need.
> - Read the paragraph very carefully to answer the question.
> - We sometimes use different words and phrases to give the same information.

2 Read the Skill box. Chose the correct options to complete the sentences. <u>Underline</u> the phrase in the text that helped you answer the questions.

1 Carla and Mason have _____ .
   a jobs at the same hotel   **b** lots of cameras   **c** different opinions about *Eye*
2 Bruno Catalano _____ .
   a makes sculptures   **b** only has one arm   **c** is from Spain
3 Elodie and Christine _____ .
   a are friends of the artist   **b** live in Marseille   **c** are on holiday
4 Günther _____ the lifesaver sculpture.
   a likes   **b** doesn't like   **c** doesn't give an opinion about
5 Helga works _____ .
   a in a school   **b** in a restaurant   **c** as a taxi driver

3 Match the words in the box with parts of the body 1–7 in the pictures on page 53.

head   foot   eye   body   leg   hand   arm

1 _____   2 _____   3 _____   4 _____   5 _____   6 _____   7 _____

Personal Best

Go to Vocabulary practice: parts of the body, page 121

4 Match the people with the opinions.

1 Carla   **a** 'I don't think it means anything.'
2 Mason   **b** 'I like it.'
3 Elodie and Christine   **c** 'I think this is really ugly.'
4 Günther   **d** 'In my opinion, that's what it means.'
5 Helga   **e** 'It's beautiful.'

> 🧩 **Text builder** **giving opinions**
>
> **Phrases:** *In my opinion, ...*   *In my view, ...*
> **Verbs:** *I think/don't think ...*   *I like/don't like ...*
> **Adjectives:** *It's beautiful/ugly/interesting/boring/strange*, etc.
>
> **Look!** We say: *I don't think it's ugly.*
> NOT *I think it isn't ugly.*

5 Read the Text builder. In pairs, describe the sculptures in the pictures and give your opinions.

I love it ...
but what is it?

There's art everywhere in our towns, cities and parks. Sometimes it's good, sometimes it's bad, but it's always interesting.

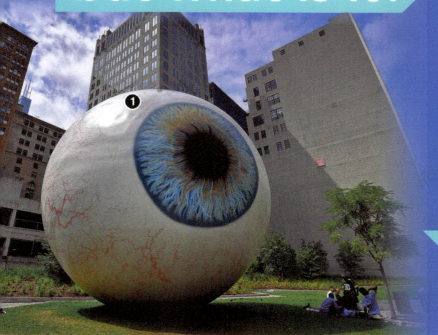

Eye

In the garden of a five-star hotel in Dallas, USA, there's a 10-metre-high eye, called *Eye*. 'It's really interesting,' says Carla, a receptionist at the hotel. 'There are cameras everywhere today, watching us. In my opinion, that's what it means.' Mason, a waiter from another hotel, doesn't agree. 'I don't think it means anything,' he says. 'It's just an eye!'

Travellers

In Marseille, France, there's an amazing sculpture by the French artist Bruno Catalano. It's a man on a journey. He only has one arm and he doesn't have a body. 'It's beautiful', say Elodie and her friend Christine, tourists from Paris. 'Perhaps it means that when we leave a place, we leave a part of us behind.'

Lifesaver fountain

This fountain in Duisburg in Germany is big and colourful. It has a person's legs, but a bird's head and feet. But what is it? And what do local people think? 'I usually like modern art,' says Günther, a taxi driver. 'But I think this is really ugly.' Helga, a teacher, disagrees. 'I like it,' she says. 'I often have lunch in a restaurant on this street. When I see the fountain, I feel happy.'

Personal Best   Write about a piece of art you like and give your opinion of it.

53

6C An unusual home

1 Match the furniture in the box with pictures a–f.

fridge table bed sofa wardrobe chair

 a
 b
 c
 d
 e
 f

Personal Best

Go to Vocabulary practice: rooms and furniture, page 122

2 In pairs, describe a room in your house. Can your partner guess the room?

A *There's a table and four chairs in this room.*　　B *Is it your kitchen?*
A *No, it's my living room!*

3 Look at the picture. Guess where Kirsten lives. Read the text and check.

Life on the water

For university students, a room in a flat or a house can be very expensive, but not for 20-year-old Kirsten Müller. Kirsten is a student at a business school in Berlin … and she lives on a boat! It's small, but it's home.

Kirsten is on the sofa in the living room. There's a small table in front of her. 'I study here every night,' she says. 'And I eat here too.' The kitchen has an electric cooker, and next to it, there's a small fridge. Kirsten cooks all her meals on the boat. 'It's perfect for me, but I can't invite lots of friends for dinner!'

The bedroom has a bed … and nothing else! All of Kirsten's clothes are in boxes under the bed because there isn't a wardrobe. Between the bedroom and the kitchen, there's a modern bathroom with a shower and a toilet.

Kirsten loves her home. It's cheap and the people on the other boats are friendly, but are there any problems? 'I don't like getting up in winter,' she says. 'It's very cold!'

4 Read the text again. Match the rooms in the box with the parts of the boat.

living room bathroom bedroom kitchen

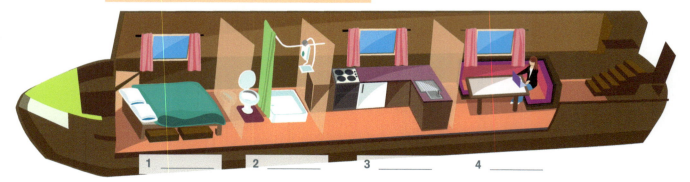

1 _____ 2 _____ 3 _____ 4 _____

5 Look at the diagram in exercise 4 again. Complete the sentences with the prepositions of place in the box. Check your answers in the text. Then read the Grammar box.

> under   between   in   on   next to   in front of

1 Kirsten is _____ the sofa.
2 There's a small table _____ her.
3 The kitchen has an electric cooker, and _____ it, there's a small fridge.
4 All of Kirsten's clothes are _____ boxes _____ the bed.
5 _____ the bedroom and the kitchen, there's a modern bathroom.

📖 **Grammar**   **prepositions of place**

There's a table **next to** the sofa.   My bedroom is **above** our living room.
My mobile phone is **in** my bag.   Luca sits **between** Carlos and Emma.
Your shoes are **under** the bed.   Your car is **in front of** our house.
My keys are **on** the table.   The cat is **behind** the sofa.

Go to Grammar practice: prepositions of place, page 101

6 ▶ 6.10   **Pronunciation:** sentence stress Listen and repeat the sentences. Pay attention to the <u>underlined</u> stressed words.

1 The <u>camera</u> is <u>under</u> my <u>bed</u>.
2 Your <u>head</u> is in <u>front</u> of the <u>TV</u>.
3 His <u>shoes</u> are <u>next</u> to the <u>sofa</u>.
4 The <u>bathroom</u> is <u>behind</u> the <u>door</u>.

7 **A** Complete the sentences with the correct prepositions of place.

1 The window is _____ the table.
2 Your keys are _____ the book.
3 The books are _____ the shelves.
4 There's a bed _____ the window and the chair.

B ▶ 6.11   In pairs, say the sentences with the correct stress. Listen, check and repeat.

8 **A** ▶ 6.12   Look at the picture and listen to the description. Find five differences between the description and the picture.

B ▶ 6.12   Compare your answers in pairs. Listen again and check.
There isn't a clock on the table. There's a lamp on the table.

Go to Communication practice: Student A page 138, Student B page 146

9 **A** Think of a room in your house. Make notes about what furniture is in it and where it is.

B In pairs, describe your room. Your partner draws it. Then check your pictures.

10 Ask and answer the questions in pairs.

1 Do you live in a house or a flat?
2 Which is your favourite room? Why?
3 Imagine your ideal bedroom/living room/kitchen. What's in it?

Personal Best   Write about your 'dream' home.

Learning Curve

6D Is there a post office near here?

1 In pairs, discuss what you usually do when you're lost.

   a Ask someone in the street for directions.
   b Go into a shop and ask for directions.
   c Look at a map.
   d Use a Sat Nav app on your phone.
   e Walk around and hope you find the place.

2 ▶ 6.13 Watch or listen to the first part of *Learning Curve*. Choose the correct words to complete the sentences.

   1 Simon has *cereal and tea / eggs, toast and coffee / eggs, toast and tea* for breakfast.
   2 He never goes to work *by car / by bike / on the underground*.
   3 Kate always says *'the underground' / 'the subway' / 'the tube'*.
   4 The man wants to find *a car park / a post office / the underground station*.

3 ▶ 6.13 Complete the conversation with phrases a–e. Watch or listen again and check.

Man	Excuse me. ¹_____
Simon	Yes, there is. ²_____
	Go straight on. ³_____
Man	⁴_____
Simon	⁵_____

   a It's on the left, near the car park.
   b Thank you very much.
   c No problem.
   d It's down the street.
   e Is there a post office around here?

⟵⟶ Conversation builder   asking for and giving directions

Asking for directions:
Excuse me.
Is there a post office near here?
Is there a post office around here?
Where's the post office?

Giving directions:
Go straight on.
Go down this street.
Turn right/left at …
It's on the right/left/corner.
It's near/next to/in front of …

4 A Read the Conversation builder. In pairs, look at the maps and ask for and give directions to the places in orange.

   A *Excuse me, where's the bank?*   **B** *Go straight on …*

B ▶ 6.14 Listen and check. Are your conversations similar?

5 ▶️ 6.15   Watch or listen to the second part of the show. Choose the correct options to answer the questions.

1   Where do the women want to go?
   a   To the cinema.
   b   To the shopping centre.
   c   To the supermarket.

2   What's the problem at the studio?
   a   There isn't any water.
   b   There isn't any tea.
   c   There isn't any electricity.

6 ▶️ 6.15   Watch or listen again. Complete the conversations with the phrases in the box.

> a problem   show me   near here   did you say   repeat that   you mean

1   **Woman 1** Is there a shopping centre
   ¹_____ ?
   Simon Yes, it's near the supermarket. Go down this street, turn right on Bethnal Green Road. Don't stop at Ebor Street. Go straight on.
   Woman 2 Sorry, ²_____ near the supermarket?

2   **Woman 1** Can you ³_____ on the map?
   Simon We're here. And there's the cinema. And there's the supermarket. The shopping centre is next to the supermarket. See?
   Woman 2 Could you ⁴_____ , please? More slowly.

3   **Kate** There's ⁵_____ , so there's no water in the kitchen or the bathroom. But there's water under the receptionist's desk! Poor Marina.
   Simon Sorry, did you say there's a problem on the street?
   ⁶_____ , a problem with the water?

🔧 **Skill   checking information**

If you don't understand what someone says, you can:
- ask him/her to repeat: *Could you repeat that, please?   Could you say that again?*
- ask him/her to speak more slowly: *Could you speak more slowly, please?*
- ask a question to check the information: *Did you say near the supermarket?   You mean, a problem with the water?*

7 **A** ▶️ 6.16   Read the Skill box. Listen and match phrases a–d with conversations 1–4. Where are the people in the situations?

a   Sorry, did you say ...?   _____
b   Sorry, could you say that again, please?   _____
c   Sorry, could you repeat that, please?   _____
d   Sorry, could you speak more slowly, please?   _____

B ▶️ 6.16   Listen again and complete the information that the people repeat.

1   Turn right at the _____ .
   Then turn _____ at
   the _____ .

2   _____ . _____ @mail.com
3   70832 _____
4   £ _____

Go to Communication practice: Student A page 139, Student B page 147

8 **A** PREPARE   In pairs, think of four places in your town. Think about how to get to the places from where you are now.

> a train station or bus stop
> a restaurant or café
> a museum or tourist attraction
> a shopping centre or supermarket

B PRACTISE   Ask for and give directions. Check the information if you don't understand anything.

C PERSONAL BEST   Swap partners and ask for and give directions to a new place. Are you more confident asking for directions in English?

Personal **Best**   Write an email to a friend with directions to your house from the bus or train station.

Grammar

1 Choose the correct options to complete the sentences.

1 On Saturday, I meet my friends _____ the shopping centre.
   a on   b under   c in

2 _____ any shelves in the living room.
   a There aren't
   b There are
   c There isn't

3 He can't _____ cakes. They're always horrible!
   a make   b to make   c makes

4 My friends live in the city. I meet _____ at the weekend.
   a they   b them   c us

5 There are _____ in the kitchen.
   a any biscuits
   b some biscuit
   c some biscuits

6 Your sunglasses are _____ to my laptop.
   a on   b in front   c next

7 A Is there a hospital in your town?
   B Yes, _____ .
   a there's
   b there is
   c there are

8 _____ drive a lorry?
   a Do you can
   b Can you
   c You can

2 Complete the conversations with the words in the box.

> aren't any can can't her
> isn't it next to on them

1 A _____ you swim?
  B Yes, I can, but there _____ a swimming pool in this town.

2 A Are there _____ restaurants near here?
  B Yes, there's an Italian restaurant _____ the supermarket on School Road.

3 A Where are my headphones? I want to use _____ .
  B They're _____ the desk.

4 A Who can speak Spanish? I _____ read this menu.
  B Give _____ to me. I know some Spanish.

5 A Selina's class is at 8.00 p.m., but there _____ any buses in the evening.
  B It's OK. I can drive _____ to the class.

3 Choose the correct options to complete the text.

A treehouse with a difference

If you want an unusual house, Jono Williams can [1] *make / makes* one for you. He's an engineer and he loves treehouses, but his new Skysphere is different – it's very small and it isn't [2] *in / under* a tree!

What's in the Skysphere?
[3] *There's / There are* a large bed, a TV and [4] *any / some* shelves. There's even a fridge for drinks [5] *between / in* the sofa! The windows are very large and Jono [6] *can / can't* see 360° around the house. There's Wi-Fi and he can [7] *use / using* his smartphone to play music and change the lights.

What does Jono do there?
Jono meets his friends at the Skysphere. They love [8] *them / it* too. They like listening to music and at night they can watch the stars.

Are there [9] *some / any* problems with Jono's house?
Only one … there [10] *isn't / aren't* a bathroom or a toilet.

Vocabulary

1 Put the words in the box in the correct columns.

> museum lamp table DVD player remote control
> head teeth park chair Sat Nav laptop desk
> police station post office face foot

Places in a town	Electronic devices	Parts of the body	Furniture

2 (Circle) the word that is different. Explain your answers.

1	toilet	bath	table	shower
2	ear	mouth	nose	hand
3	school	supermarket	restaurant	café
4	bank	kitchen	bedroom	living room
5	chair	arm	fridge	wardrobe
6	walking	reading	swimming	cycling
7	sing	speak	travel	call
8	DVD player	shelves	computer	Sat Nav

3 Choose the correct options to complete the sentences.

1 My city has two _____ .
   a wardrobes   b hospitals   c bathrooms
2 What time does the bus _____ in the city centre?
   a arrive   b travel   c go out
3 Her _____ is long and brown.
   a eye   b hair   c mouth
4 There's a large _____ in the living room.
   a bath   b leg   c sofa
5 She always uses _____ to listen to music on the bus.
   a earphones   b TV   c shelves
6 A Where's the _____ ?   B It's in the car.
   a museum   b toilet   c Sat Nav
7 Is there any cheese in the _____ ?
   a shower   b fridge   c DVR
8 At the weekend, I like _____ at the cinema.
   a dancing   b sleeping   c watching films

4 Complete the conversations with the words in the boxes.

bedroom cooker windows desk nightclub cooking

Ama Hi, Ed! How are you? Do you like your new flat?
Ed No, not really. It's above a noisy ^{1}_____ .
Ama Oh no! Is it big?
Ed No, it's very small. In the ^{2}_____ , there's only a bed and a ^{3}_____ , and there aren't any ^{4}_____ in the bathroom.
Ama How's the kitchen? I know you like ^{5}_____ .
Ed It's dirty and the ^{6}_____ is very old ... but it's a good flat.
Ama What's good about it?
Ed It's cheap!

call station office speak drive stop

Sam Excuse me. Do you ^{7}_____ English?
Fran Yes, I do.
Sam Where's the bus ^{8}_____ ?
Fran It's in front of the post ^{9}_____ , but there aren't any buses today.
Sam OK. Is there a train ^{10}_____ near here?
Fran Yes, but it's a long walk. I can ^{11}_____ you there if you want.
Sam No thanks, I can ^{12}_____ a taxi.

Personal Best

Lesson 5A
Write one positive and one negative sentence about your abilities.

Lesson 6A
Name five places in your town.

Lesson 5B
Name four electronic devices that you use.

Lesson 6A
Write three questions to find out what there is in a friend's town.

Lesson 5C
Name two activities that you like doing and two activities that you don't like doing.

Lesson 6B
Write your opinion of a famous building.

Lesson 5C
Write four sentences with different object pronouns.

Lesson 6B
Name five parts of the body that you have two of.

Lesson 5D

Write four sentences to describe yourself.

Lesson 6C
Name four things in your house and describe where they are.

Lesson 5D

Say why you like/don't like your town/city using *because*.

Lesson 6D

Write directions from the classroom to a shop, café, school or bus stop.

All in the past

7A   When they were young

1   Match the jobs in the box with pictures a–f.

musician   politician   film director   writer   footballer   fashion model

Personal Best

Go to Vocabulary practice: celebrities, page 123

2   In pairs, describe celebrities. Can your partner guess who it is?

A   *She's a tennis player. She's American. She's very good!*   **B**   *Is it Serena Williams?*

3   A   Read the introduction of the text. Match the blue sign with one of the people a–e.

B   Read the rest of the text. Match the other people with descriptions 1–4 and write their names on the blue signs. Check their names on page 139.

ENGLISH HERITAGE
Sir
ALFRED
HITCHCOCK
1899–1980
Film Director
lived here
1926–1939

London's
famous houses

London was home to lots of famous people from all over the world. Who were they and where were their houses? It's easy – just look for the blue signs on the buildings!

1869–1948
Lived here as
a law student

1 He was a famous Indian politician, but he was also a student in London for three years. He was a vegetarian and in the 19th century it wasn't easy to find good vegetarian food in the city.

1890–1976
Writer
Lived here
1934–1941

3 This British writer wasn't from London, but she was here for seven years. Her crime stories were very popular around the world, and you probably know her famous detective – Hercule Poirot.

1945–1981
Singer and musician
Lived here
1972

2 In 1972, London was home to this Jamaican singer and his band. The musicians weren't famous then, but a year later their song *Stir It Up* was a big hit.

1853–1890
Artist
Lived here
1873–1874

4 This was the Dutch artist's home when he was 19 years old. He was in love with the owner's daughter, Eugenie. But was she interested in him? No, she wasn't!

4 A Complete the sentences with the words in the box. Check your answers in the text.

> was (x2)   were (x2)   wasn't   weren't

1 Where _____ their houses?
2 He _____ a famous Indian politician.
3 It _____ easy to find good vegetarian food.

4 The musicians _____ famous then.
5 Her crime stories _____ very popular.
6 _____ she interested in him?

B Complete the rules. Then read the Grammar box.

1 The past simple forms of *is/isn't* = _____ / _____ .
2 The past simple forms of *are/aren't* = _____ / _____ .

📖 **Grammar**   **past simple: *be***

Positive:	Negative:	Questions:	Short answers:	
He **was** a musician.	I **wasn't** an actor.	**Was** she a writer?	Yes, she **was**.	No, she **wasn't**.
They **were** singers.	You **weren't** famous.	**Were** you happy?	Yes, we **were**.	No, we **weren't**.

Go to Grammar practice: past simple: *be*, page 102

5 A ▶ 7.3   **Pronunciation:** *was/were* Listen and repeat the question and answer.
How are *was* and *were* pronounced?

A *Where were you yesterday?*   **B** *I was at work.*

B In pairs, ask and answer the question *Where were you ...?* with the times in the boxes.
Pay attention to the pronunciation of *was* and *were*.

A *Where were you at 7.30 this morning?*   **B** *I was on the bus. I always go to work early. What about you?*
A *I was in bed!*

> at 7.30 this morning   yesterday morning   yesterday at 2.00 p.m.   yesterday evening

Go to Communication practice: Student A page 139, Student B page 147

6 ▶ 7.4   Complete the sentences with the correct form of *was* or *were*. Listen and check.

When they were young

- Singer Justin Timberlake and actor Ryan Gosling ¹_____ presenters on a children's TV show when they ²_____ young.

- In 1990, J.K. Rowling ³_____ an English teacher in Portugal, but she ⁴_____ happy there. Seven years later, she ⁵_____ famous all over the world as the writer of the *Harry Potter* books.

- Actors and film directors Matt Damon and Ben Affleck ⁶_____ at school together, but they ⁷_____ in the same class.

- Athlete Usain Bolt ⁸_____ interested in cricket and football at school. His teachers ⁹_____ surprised because he ¹⁰_____ a very, very fast runner!

7 In pairs, ask and answer questions about when you were young. Use the ideas below.

A *What was the name of your first teacher?*   **B** *Mrs Fuentes. She was really nice. What about you?*

1 What / the name of your first teacher?
2 / you a good student?
3 / you in a big class?
4 Who / your best friend?

5 What celebrities / popular when you / a child?
6 What films / popular?
7 What / your favourite TV programmes?
8 What / your favourite food?

Personal Best Think of someone famous that you like. Write a paragraph about their life when they were young.

Learning Curve

7B I was there in July

1 Order the months from 1–12.

☐ April   ☐ August   ☐ December   ☐ February
☒ 1 January ☐ July   ☐ June   ☐ March
☐ May   ☐ November   ☐ October   ☐ September

Personal Best

2 Look at the calendar. Match days a–f with dates 1–6.

1 the thirty-first of May _____   4 the twelfth of May _____
2 the twentieth of May _____   5 the first of May _____
3 the twenty-eighth of May _____ 6 the third of May _____

Go to Vocabulary practice: months and ordinals, page 124

May

1 a	2	3 b	4	5	6	7
8	9	10	11	12 c	13	14
15	16	17	18	19	20 d	21
22	23	24	25	26	27	28 e
29	30	31 f				

3 Ask and answer the questions in pairs.

1 What's the date today?   3 What's your favourite month?
2 When's your birthday?   4 When was the last public holiday?

4 A Look at the picture. What do you know about Shakespeare?

B Complete the text with the words in the box.

> April *Hamlet* plays writer

> William Shakespeare was a famous British ¹_____ . He was born on
> 26 ²_____ 1564 and he died in April 1616. His ³_____ are popular
> all over the world. They include *Romeo and Juliet*, ⁴_____ and *Othello*.

5 ▶ 7.7   Watch or listen to the first part of *Learning Curve*. Are the sentences true (T) or false (F)?

1 Shakespeare's plays are only about British people.   _____
2 The Globe Theatre was Shakespeare's first theatre.   _____
3 'Shakespeare in the Park' in New York is very expensive.   _____
4 You can read Shakespeare's plays in 80 different languages. _____

🔧 **Skill**   listening for dates

It's sometimes important to listen for specific years and months.
• Listen carefully because some months sound similar: *September, November* and *December*.
• Years are usually divided into two numbers: *1990 = nineteen ninety, 2008 = twenty oh eight*.
  For years after 2000, we sometimes use the whole number: *2009 = two thousand and nine*.
• We use ordinals to talk about centuries (100 years): *1900–1999 = the twentieth century*.

6 ▶ 7.7   Read the Skill box. Watch or listen again. Complete the texts with the correct information.

The Globe Theatre was Shakespeare's first
theatre. It was here in London during the
¹_____ and ²_____ centuries, from
³_____ to about ⁴_____ . This theatre
looks just like the old Globe.

Every year, from ⁵_____ to ⁶_____ ,
there's a Shakespeare festival in Central Park
in New York City. It's called 'Shakespeare in the
Park'. 1,800 people can see a Shakespeare play
at the Delacorte Theater for free!

7 ▶ 7.8   Watch or listen to the rest of the show. Match the people with sentences 1–4.

Marty

Elizabeth and Henry

Zhang

1   This person likes plays about love. _____
2   This person works at a theatre.   _____

3   This person doesn't like Shakespeare. _____
4   This person likes plays about history. _____

8 ▶ 7.8   Watch or listen again. Answer the questions with months or years.
1   When does Marty come to New York?   _____ and _____
2   When were Elizabeth and Henry in Cambridge?   _____
3   When was *A Midsummer Night's Dream* in Beijing?   _____
4   When was *Henry IV* at the Hong Kong Arts Festival?   _____

9   Ask and answer the questions in pairs.

Do you ever go to the theatre?   Which Shakespeare plays do you know?

Which types of plays do you like?   Do you like Shakespeare? Why/Why not?

10 ▶ 7.9   Listen to Penny's sentence and look at the linked words. Pay attention to how the sounds join together.

A lot‿of people‿are here‿in the queue for theatre tickets.

┉┉ **Listening builder**   **linking consonants and vowels**

When a word ends in a consonant sound, and the next word starts with a vowel sound, we usually link the sounds together.
Hamlet‿is‿about‿a prince‿in Denmark.
I'm‿Elizabeth‿and this‿is my husband, Henry.
Sometimes the plays‿are‿in‿English‿and Chinese.

11 ▶ 7.10   Read the Listening builder. Then listen and complete the sentences.
1   Hi, my name's Lucas _____ _____ _____ _____ .
2   In _____ _____ _____ _____ New York City for the first time.
3   The play _____ _____ _____ _____ king.
4   She was born on the _____ _____ _____ , 1999.
5   I like *Hamlet*, but I _____ _____ _____ the story.

12   Look at the pictures. Discuss the questions in pairs.

1   When was the last time you were at a theatre/a cinema/a concert?
2   Which play/film/band was it?
3   Was it good? Why/Why not?

Personal **Best**   Write a description of your favourite play or film. Where does it happen? What's it about?

7C Famous decades

1 Match the decades in the box with a–f.

the nineties   the twenty-tens   the seventies   the noughties   the sixties   the eighties

 a    b    c    d    e    f

2 Discuss the questions in pairs.

I was born in the eighties. What about you?

1 In which decade were you born?
2 Which decade has the best music and fashion, in your opinion?
3 Which was your favourite decade? Why?

3 ▶ 7.11   In pairs, complete the quiz with the years in the box. Listen and check.

1969   1973   1985   1991   2004   2012

The Decades Quiz

On 4 February ¹_____ , Mark Zuckerberg started Facebook from his bedroom at university. He wanted 500 people to join. Now, more than 1.5 billion people use it!

In ⁴_____ , Korean singer Psy danced *Gangnam Style* all over the world. The song was number 1 in 37 countries. Did you watch the video?

 On 20 July ²_____ , Neil Armstrong and Buzz Aldrin walked on the moon. 600 million people watched on TV or listened on the radio.

 On 30 November ⁵_____ , the USA and Norway played in the first Women's Football World Cup final in China. The result was a 2–1 win for the USA.

In April ³_____ , Coca-Cola® tried a new recipe for their drink. People didn't like the flavour, and three months later, the original Coca-Cola was back in the shops.

On 3 April ⁶_____ , Martin Cooper from Motorola called Joel Engel on the world's first mobile phone. Joel quickly stopped the call because he wasn't happy. He worked for rival company AT&T!

4 Read the quiz again. Write the past simple form of verbs 1–8.

1 start _____   3 watch _____   5 dance _____   7 call _____
2 walk _____   4 try _____   6 play _____   8 stop _____

5 **A** Look at the verbs in exercise 4 again and complete the rules.

1 We usually add the letters _____ to verbs to make the past simple form.
2 If the verb ends in -*e*, we add the letter _____ to make the past simple form.
3 If the verb ends in consonant + *y*, we remove the *y* and add the letters _____ to make the past simple form.
4 If the verb ends in consonant + vowel + consonant, we double the last consonant and add _____.

B Complete the sentences from the text to make the negative and question forms of the past simple. Does the main verb change form? Read the Grammar box.

1 People _____ like the flavour.   2 _____ you watch the video?

📖 **Grammar** past simple: regular verbs

Positive:
*600 million people **watched** on TV.*
*Coca-Cola **tried** a new recipe.*

Negative:
*They **didn't call** on a smartphone.*
*Brazil **didn't play** in the final.*

Questions and short answers:
*Did you **try** the new drink?*
*Yes, I **did**. No, I **didn't**.*

Personal Best

Go to Grammar practice: past simple: regular verbs, page 102

6 ▶ 7.13 Complete the text with the past simple form of the verbs in brackets. Listen and check.

Were the nineties the best decade for films?

My brother ¹_____ (study) films at university and he thinks the nineties were the best decade for cinema. So last week, I ²_____ (decide) to watch the film *Titanic* for the first time. It was in the cinema 20 years ago, but I was only two then.
I ³_____ (love) it … but it's a sad story. It's about a real disaster that ⁴_____ (happen) in 1912 in the Atlantic Ocean. Thousands of people ⁵_____ (die) because the ship ⁶_____ (not carry) enough lifeboats.
After that, I ⁷_____ (want) to see more films from the nineties. So at the weekend, I ⁸_____ (watch) *Jurassic Park*, *Forrest Gump* and *Pulp Fiction*. On Monday, it was *Toy Story*, and last night, I ⁹_____ (start) watching *The Matrix* … but I ¹⁰_____ (not finish) it because at 1.00 a.m. I ¹¹_____ (need) to go to bed. My brother was right – films from the nineties are amazing!

7 Complete the time expressions with the words in the box. Check your answers in the text in exercise 6.

in   ago   last (x2)   on   at (x2)

1 20 years _____
2 _____ week
3 _____ 1912
4 _____ the weekend
5 _____ night
6 _____ Monday
7 _____ 1.00 a.m.

Personal Best

Go to Vocabulary practice: time expressions, page 124

8 A ▶ 7.15 **Pronunciation:** *-ed* endings Listen and repeat the sentences from the text.
Pay attention to the *-ed* endings in **bold**: /d/, /t/ and /ɪd/.

1 /d/   lov**ed**   I lov**ed** it.
2 /t/   watch**ed**   I watch**ed** *Jurassic Park*.
3 /ɪd/   need**ed**   I need**ed** to go to bed.

B ▶ 7.16 Write the verbs in the box in the correct columns. Listen, check and repeat.

danced   wanted   played   tried   walked   visited

/d/	/t/	/ɪd/

Go to Communication practice: Student A page 139, Student B page 147

9 A In pairs, ask and answer the questions with the past simple form of the verbs. Write your partner's answers in the table.

A *When did you last watch a film on DVD?*
B *I watched a film on DVD about a year ago.*

When did you last …	Answers
1 watch / a film on DVD?	
2 study / for an exam?	
3 cook / chicken?	
4 play / a musical instrument?	
5 call / a friend on the phone?	

When was the last time you …	Answers
6 use / a computer?	
7 dance / with friends?	
8 relax / at home?	
9 talk / to a neighbour?	
10 listen / to the radio?	

B Tell the class about your partner.

Marco watched a film on DVD about a year ago.

Personal Best Choose six different time expressions and write a true past simple sentence for each one.

7D A weekend away

1 In pairs, order the pictures from 1–6 to make a story about Elena and her father's trip to Oxford.

2 Read Elena's email and check the order of the pictures in exercise 1.

To: Becky Stewart

Subject: My weekend

Hi Becky,

How are things? I hope you're well.

Did I tell you about last weekend? I visited my sister Hannah. She lives in Oxford now. I wanted to go on my own … but Dad decided to come with me!

We travelled by train on Saturday. We arrived in Oxford and Hannah was at the train station. In the afternoon, we explored the city. First, we walked round the university. It was beautiful, but Dad stopped to take hundreds of photos! Then we visited an art gallery. Dad studied every painting and looked at every sculpture – we were there for hours! After that, Hannah and I wanted to go shopping, but Dad wanted to visit a museum. It was so boring!

It was a disaster! This weekend, I want to stay at home, or go away without Dad!

See you soon.

Elena

3 A Read the email again. Are the sentences true (T) or false (F)?

1 Elena and her dad travelled to Oxford. _____
2 They stayed in Oxford for a week. _____
3 Elena's dad didn't like the university. _____
4 They explored the university on foot. _____
5 They didn't stay in the art gallery for a long time. _____
6 Hannah and Elena didn't want to visit the museum. _____

B Look at the email again and answer the questions. Then read the Skill box.

1 How does Elena start her email?
2 How does she ask how her friend is?
3 How does she introduce her news?
4 How does she finish her email?

Skill | writing informal emails

We write informal emails to friends and people we know well.

• Start the email in a friendly way: *Hi …, Hello …*
• Ask about the person: *How are you? How are things? I hope you're well.*
• Say why you are writing: *Did I tell you about …? I wanted to tell/ask you …*
• Finish the email in a friendly way: *See you soon, Bye for now, Take care.*

4 Complete the email with the words in the box.

> hope   how   hello   tell   now

To: George Hawkins
Subject: Fantastic weekend

¹_____ George,
²_____ are you? I ³_____ you and the family are well.
I wanted to ⁴_____ you about last weekend. My daughter Elena and I travelled to Oxford.
My other daughter, Hannah, moved there a few months ago, so we stayed with her.
On Saturday, we walked into town. First, we explored the university. It was very interesting. Elena loved all the old buildings! Then we visited an art gallery. We were there for hours – the girls didn't want to leave! After that, we looked around the museum. I was quite tired, but the girls really enjoyed it. It was a great weekend. I think Elena wants to do it again soon.
Bye for ⁵_____ .
Frank

5 Discuss the questions in pairs.

1 Who is Frank?
2 What differences are there between Frank and Elena's emails?
3 Do you enjoy visiting art galleries and museums? Why/Why not?

6 Order sentences a–c from 1–3. Check your answers in the email in exercise 4.

a ☐ After that, we looked around the museum.
b ☐ First, we explored the university.
c ☐ Then we visited an art gallery.

◄◄► **Text builder**   **sequencers**

We can show the order of events with *First*, *Then* and *After that*:
First, we walked into town.   *Then* we visited the university.   *After that*, we explored the centre.
Look! We usually use a comma after *First* and *After that*.

7 Read the Text builder. Then write sentences in the past simple with sequencers.

First, we listened to some music. Then we cooked dinner …

1 We / listen to / some music. We / cook / dinner. We / watch / a film.
2 She / visit / her sister. She / call / her mum. She / talk to / her dad.
3 I / walk to / my friend's house. We / study / English together. We / play / football.

8 A **PREPARE** Think of a weekend when you were somewhere interesting.
Make notes about what happened. Think about:

- where you travelled to
- how you travelled
- who was with you
- where you stayed
- the places that you visited
- if you enjoyed it

Use these regular verbs to help you:

> visit travel play walk watch listen to wait love
> cook explore stay talk enjoy need want try

B **PRACTISE** Write an email to a friend about your weekend.
Use the Skill box and Text builder to help you.

C **PERSONAL BEST** Swap your email with your partner. Does your partner use the past simple correctly? Can you correct any mistakes?

Personal Best   Write about a day when you visited a lot of places, like Elena's day in Oxford.

Travel

8A   Incredible journeys

1   Complete the sentences with the verbs in the box.

get lost   book   fly   miss   ride   take

1   Some of my friends _____ motorbikes to work.

3   I sometimes _____ the bus because I get up late.

5   I never _____ because I don't like it!

2   I always _____ train tickets early to get a good price.

4   If I go out at night, I usually _____ a taxi home.

6   I often _____ in a new town.

Go to Vocabulary practice: travel verbs, page 125

2   In pairs, say the sentences in exercise 1. Decide if they are true or false for your partner.

A   *Some of my friends ride motorbikes to work.*   B   *False.*
A   *You're right. All my friends drive to work.*

3   Look at the title and the picture. In pairs, guess what the story is about. Read the text and check.

Around the world *for love*

In January 2001, Ian Johnstone from Yorkshire in the UK went to work in Australia for a year, but his girlfriend Amy stayed at home. It was difficult to be so far away from her and after six months, Ian planned to visit her. He wanted to ask her to marry him, but he didn't tell her about his plans … it was a surprise visit!

Ian booked a flight and in July he flew from Sydney to London, with a stop in Singapore. But he didn't know about Amy's plans. She also wanted to surprise Ian with a visit, and at that exact moment, she was also on a plane … to Australia!

When Ian arrived in London, he bought some flowers and took the train to Yorkshire. Amy wasn't at home, so Ian waited for her. At the same time, Amy arrived at Ian's flat in Sydney. When his flatmate told her that Ian was 17,000 km away in England, Amy thought that it was a joke!

It wasn't possible for Ian or Amy to change their tickets, so they didn't see each other. But the story had a happy ending. Ian called Amy and asked her to marry him. And what did she say? She said 'yes', of course!

Amy Dolby
Ian Johnstone

UK
London
SINGAPORE
AUSTRALIA
Sydney

4 Are the sentences true (T) or false (F)? Read the text again and check.

1 Ian went to Australia with Amy. ____
2 He wanted to see his girlfriend. ____
3 Amy lived in London. ____
4 She travelled to Australia to see Ian. ____
5 They changed their tickets. ____
6 Amy didn't want to marry Ian. ____

5 A Look at the past simple verbs in **bold** in the sentence from the text. Which verb is regular and which is irregular?

Ian **booked** a flight and in July he **flew** from Sydney to London.

B Find the past simple form of the irregular verbs in the text. Then read the Grammar box.

1 go _____ 2 fly _*flew*_ 3 buy _____ 4 take _____ 5 think _____ 6 say _____

📖 **Grammar**   **past simple: irregular verbs**

Positive:	Negative:	Questions:	Short answers:
Ian **went** to work in Australia.	Ian **didn't go** to work in Singapore.	**Did** Ian **go** home?	Yes, he **did**.
He **flew** to London.	He **didn't fly** to Sydney.	**Did** he **fly** alone?	No, he **didn't**.
He **bought** some flowers.	He **didn't buy** chocolate.	**Did** he **buy** a ring?	

Personal Best

Go to Grammar practice: past simple: irregular verbs, page 103

6 Complete the text with the past simple form of the verbs in brackets.

Around the world – on foot! 👣 👣 👣 👣
This is Jean Béliveau, a Canadian who walked around the world, through 64 countries in 11 years!

When [1]_____ he _____ (leave)?
Jean [2]_____ (leave) his home on 18 August 2000, and he [3]_____ (not get) home until 2011.
His wife, Luce, [4]_____ (not go) with him, but she [5]_____ (fly) to meet him eleven times.
Where [6]_____ he _____ (sleep)?
He [7]_____ (sleep) in people's homes, parks, schools, hospitals – and even in a police station!
People also [8]_____ (buy) him food and drink.
Why [9]_____ he _____ (do) it?
He [10]_____ (do) it because he wanted people to know about children's lives in other countries.

7 A ▶ 8.3   **Pronunciation: irregular past simple verbs** Listen and repeat the past simple verbs. Pay attention to the vowel sounds /ɒ/, /ɔː/ and /əʊ/.

1 /ɒ/ got lost
2 /ɔː/ bought thought
3 /əʊ/ rode drove

B ▶ 8.4   Underline the words in the sentences with the same vowel sounds. Listen, check and repeat.

1 I got on the bus.
2 We all bought a ticket.
3 I rode home on my bike.
4 He lost his new watch.
5 I thought it was a horse.
6 She drove to my home.

Go to Communication practice: Student A page 140, Student B page 148

8 A ▶ 8.5   Read Leanne's plans for a holiday to Croatia last summer. Then listen and correct the information with what really happened.

B In pairs, make sentences about Leanne's trip.

She didn't fly from Manchester. She flew from London.

9 Think about a holiday or journey. In pairs, ask and answer the questions in the boxes.

My trip to Croatia
24 July: fly from Manchester to Dubrovnik
30 July: take bus to Split
5 August: sail to Šolta
10 August: take train to Zagreb and fly home
Activities: eat local food, swim in the sea, take photos … fall in love?

Where did you go?   How did you travel?   What did you do?
When did you go?   Who did you go with?   Did you have a good time?

Personal Best   Write about your partner's holiday or journey from exercise 9.

8B Crazy weather!

1 Match the weather phrases in the box with pictures a–d on page 71.

> It's cold.   It's sunny.   It's raining.   It's windy.

Go to Vocabulary practice: weather and seasons, page 126

2 In pairs, talk about the seasons in your country. Use *love/like/don't like/hate*.

I don't like autumn because it rains and it's cold and windy.

> **Skill** | **understanding the main idea**
>
> **When you see a text for the first time, try to understand the main idea quickly.**
> • Look at the title and pictures.
> • Read the first line of each paragraph.
> • Use this information to understand what the text is about.

3 **A** Read the Skill box. Then read the title and the highlighted sentences on page 71. Tick (✔) the main idea.

a Robbie had lots of problems with transport in Germany. ☐
b Robbie went on holiday and the weather changed a lot. ☐
c Robbie was in Berlin in the summer, but it snowed all week. ☐
d Robbie didn't like the weather in Germany, so he went to Ireland. ☐

B Read the whole text and check.

4 Are the sentences true (T) or false (F)? Read the text again and check.

1 Robbie went to Berlin with his girlfriend. _____
2 They had ice cream in Viktoria Park. _____
3 They waited on a train for three hours. _____
4 It rained at the Television Tower. _____
5 They didn't go to the concert because it snowed. _____
6 They arrived at the airport late and missed the flight. _____

5 Match the halves to make sentences from the text. Do the modifiers in **bold** come before or after the adjectives?

1 When we got off the plane, it was **very**
2 When we got to the park, it was **quite**
3 And in the afternoon, it was **really**
4 The views were**n't very**

a cold.
b good.
c windy.
d hot and sunny.

> **Text builder** | **modifiers**
>
> We use modifiers before an adjective to make the meaning stronger or less strong:
> | really/very | It was **really** sunny. The film was **very** exciting. |
> | quite | The museum was **quite** interesting. |
> | not very | The food was**n't very** good. |

6 Read the Text builder. Then write sentences with the words and a modifier.

The weather today is very hot.

1 the weather today / hot
2 the *Star Wars* films / exciting
3 I think English / difficult
4 public transport in my country / expensive
5 my street / noisy
6 people in my city / friendly

7 In pairs, talk about your last trip or holiday. What was the weather like?

Last year, I visited Morocco. It was very hot and sunny in the day, and really cold at night.

Travel
news

Four Seasons In One Week

Robbie Irwin

Monday 12 March

My girlfriend and I arrived in Berlin today on holiday. We thought Germany was cold in March, so we only brought winter clothes, but we had a surprise. When we got off the plane, it was very hot and sunny! So this afternoon, we went to the shops and bought shorts and T-shirts and walked around the city centre. I even had an ice cream!

Wednesday 14 March

Today we decided to visit Viktoria Park, but the weather changed. It was warm when we left the hotel, so we wore our new shorts and T-shirts. But when we got to the park, it was quite cold. And in the afternoon, it was really windy. We decided to visit Museum Island, so we took a train back into the city … but a tree fell on the tracks, and we didn't move for three hours! After that, we went back to the hotel, changed our clothes and had dinner in a restaurant.

Thursday 15 March

The weather here is crazy – this morning it was sunny again! We decided to visit the famous Television Tower. It's over 350m tall and I wanted to take some photos of the city. But when we got to the top of the tower, it was cloudy and it started to rain – the views weren't very good. We bought some umbrellas and went to see a concert. When we came out – guess what? It was warm and sunny again!

Saturday 17 March

I can't believe it – it's 11.00 p.m. and we're still in Berlin Airport! It's really cold and it snowed all day. We took a taxi to the airport and when we arrived, we saw that there were no flights. The next flight is tomorrow morning at 7.00 a.m.

Sunday 18 March

Finally, we're back home in Ireland. We had bad luck with the weather, but we had a great trip and we loved Berlin.

a

b

c

d

 Personal Best   Write a paragraph about the weather in your town or city in different seasons.

8C Then and now

1 Match the words in the box with the parts of the picture 1–6.

| sky   field   forest   mountain   river   tree |

1 _____   4 _____
2 _____   5 _____
3 _____   6 _____

Go to Vocabulary practice: nature, page 127

2 Discuss the questions in pairs.

1 Which country is the picture in exercise 1?
2 What nature can you see out of the window?
3 Do you prefer beaches, mountains or forests? Why?

3 Read the introduction to a radio show. Answer the questions.

1 How many people live in Shenzhen? _____   3 What's her job? _____
2 Where does Liu Jiang live now? _____   4 When was she last in Shenzhen? _____

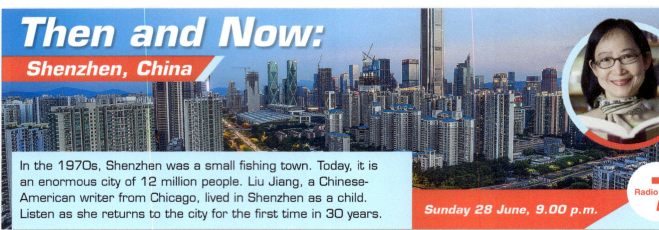

Then and Now:
Shenzhen, China

In the 1970s, Shenzhen was a small fishing town. Today, it is an enormous city of 12 million people. Liu Jiang, a Chinese-American writer from Chicago, lived in Shenzhen as a child. Listen as she returns to the city for the first time in 30 years.

Sunday 28 June, 9.00 p.m.

Radio **7**

4 ▶ 8.8   Listen to the radio show. Tick (✔) the things that Shenzhen had 30 years ago and has today.

	Fields	Forest	Tall buildings	River	Train station	Airport	University
Shenzhen 30 years ago							
Shenzhen today							

5 A ▶ 8.8   Match the halves to make sentences and questions. Listen again and check.

1 **There were** fields   a or buses?
2 **There was** a forest   b here before.
3 **There weren't** any cars   c – everyone had bicycles.
4 **Was there** public transport   d to travel around the country?
5 **Were there** any trains   e where we played.
6 **There wasn't** a university   f around the town.

B Look at the words in **bold** in sentences 1–6 again. Choose the correct options to complete the rules. Then read the Grammar box.

1 We use *there was* and *there were* to talk about *the present / the past*.
2 We use *there was* and *there wasn't* with *singular / plural* nouns.
3 We use *there were* and *there weren't* with *singular / plural* nouns.

📖 **Grammar** *there was/were*

Positive:	Negative:	Questions	Short answers:
There was a train station.	*There wasn't an airport.*	*Was there a university?*	*Yes, there was.* *No, there wasn't.*
There were lots of trees.	*There weren't any cars.*	*Were there any shops?*	*Yes, there were.* *No, there weren't.*

Go to Grammar practice: *there was/were*, page 103

6 Complete the text with the correct forms of *there was/were*.

This is Pompeii in Italy. In AD 79, a volcano destroyed the city. But what was life like for the 20,000 people that lived there before? ¹_____ about 200 cafés in the town. They sold eggs, cheese, bread and fruit. ²_____ also a market.
Children did lessons outside or at home, so ³_____ any school buildings. ⁴_____ some doctors, but ⁵_____ a hospital.
⁶_____ a big amphitheatre, where ⁷_____ plays and concerts. And of course, ⁸_____ gladiators!

7 A ▶ 8.10 **Pronunciation:** sentence stress Listen and repeat the questions and short answers. Pay attention to the <u>underlined</u> stressed words.

1 Was there a <u>train station</u>?   <u>Yes</u>, there <u>was</u>.
2 Was there an <u>airport</u>?   <u>No</u>, there <u>wasn't</u>.
3 Were there any <u>trees</u>?   <u>Yes</u>, there <u>were</u>.
4 Were there any <u>cars</u>?   <u>No</u>, there <u>weren't</u>.

B ▶ 8.11 In pairs, ask and answer questions 1–4 about Pompeii. Remember to stress the correct words. Listen, check and repeat.

1 Were there any cafés?   3 Were there any school buildings?
2 Was there a market?   4 Was there a hospital?

Go to Communication practice: Student A page 140, Student B page 148

8 In pairs, look at the pictures and talk about Oxford Street in London in the past. Use the words in the box and your own ideas.

buses   road   shops   horses and carriages   tall buildings   bus stops   street lights   taxis

There weren't any buses in the 19th century.

Oxford Street, 19th century   Oxford Street, now

9 How is your town or city different from the past? In pairs, talk about the differences.
There was a cinema on Panama Street, but now there's a supermarket.

8D A trip to Canada

1 Ask and answer the questions in pairs.

1 Why do you usually travel?
   a for work or study   **b** to visit friends or family   **c** to go on holiday   **d** other
2 How do you prefer to travel? Why?
   a to take the train   **b** to fly   **c** to drive   **d** other
3 How do you usually book your tickets when you travel?
   a online   **b** on the phone   **c** at a travel agent's   **d** other

2 A ▶ 8.12 Watch or listen to the first part of *Learning Curve*. Answer the questions.

1 Why does Marc want to travel?
2 How does he prefer to travel?
3 How does he book the tickets?

B ▶ 8.12 Are the sentences true (T) or false (F)? Watch or listen again and check.

1 Marc works with technology. _____
2 He never buys tickets online. _____
3 He loves flying. _____
4 Clarisse is Marc's friend. _____
5 It's hot and sunny in California. _____
6 The journey to Montreal is 11 hours. _____

3 ▶ 8.13 Complete the questions with the words in the box. Listen and check.

| arrive   how   leave   when   return |

1 **Clarisse** _____ do you want to leave?
   Marc   March 11.
2 **Clarisse** When would you like to _____ ?
   Marc   March 21.
3 **Marc**   What time does the train _____ ?
   Clarisse The train leaves from New York at 8.15 a.m.
4 **Marc**   And when does it _____ in Montreal?
   Clarisse 7.11 p.m.
5 **Marc**   So, _____ much is it?
   Clarisse It's $138 for a return ticket.

Conversation builder   buying a ticket

Customer:
I'd like a single/return ticket to …
What time does the train/bus/flight leave?
What time/When does it arrive?
How much is it?

Assistant:
What kind of ticket would you like?
Would you like a single or return ticket?
When do you want to return/leave?
It's … for a single/return ticket.

4 Read the Conversation builder. Then in pairs, make conversations to buy the tickets.

A *I'd like a single ticket to Newcastle, please.*   **B** *When would you like to leave?*

Ticket type: SINGLE	Date: 14 JULY
Adults: ONE	Time: 12.05
From: LONDON KING'S CROSS	Arrival: 14.55
To: NEWCASTLE	Price: £65.00

OUTBOUND	RETURN
Flight: RAX3498	Flight: RAX9912
Departing from: Frankfurt	Departing from: Marrakesh
21 September 10.00	5 October 12.35
Arriving at: Marrakesh	Arriving at: Frankfurt
21 September 14.45	5 October 17.10
	Price: €345.00

5 A ▶ 8.14 Watch or listen to the second part of the show.
Do you think Marc enjoyed his trip? Why/Why not?

B ▶ 8.14 Choose the correct options to complete the sentences.
Watch or listen again to check.

1 Marc asks Clarisse about _____ .
  a places to eat   b places to stay   c public transport
2 The Wi-Fi in Montreal isn't good when _____ .
  a it snows   b it rains   c it's windy
3 On his trip, Marc helped people with their _____ .
  a coffee and sandwiches   b French   c Wi-Fi

6 ▶ 8.15 Listen to the phrases from the conversations. Are they for starting or ending a phone call?

1
> Hello, *Bon Voyage Travel*. This is Clarisse.

2
> Thanks. Goodbye.

3
> Hello, my name is Marc Kim. I'm Penny's friend.

4
> Thanks for calling.

🔧 **Skill** **starting and ending a phone call at work**

When you speak on the telephone, remember to give important information and be polite.
- When you answer the phone, say *Hello* and identify yourself or your company: *Hello, Learning Curve. Hello, this is Clarisse / Clarisse speaking.*
- When you call someone, say who you are: *Hello, this is … , My name's …*
- When the conversation finishes, thank the person who called and say goodbye: *Thanks for calling. Thanks for your call.*

7 ▶ 8.16 Complete the conversations with the missing words. Listen and check.

Brad Hello, *Easy Travel*. Brad ¹_____ .
Jenny Hi, ²_____ is Jenny Foster. I'd like a single ticket to Seoul from Sydney, please.
…
Brad OK, Jenny. You leave on 15 June at 08.15 and you arrive in Seoul at 17.05.
Jenny Thanks very much.
Brad You're welcome. Thanks for your ³_____ .
Jenny ⁴_____ .

Go to Communication practice: Student A page 140, Student B page 148

8 A PREPARE Choose a type of transport and write down the information.

train

bus

plane

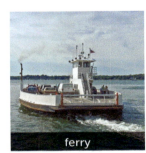
ferry

- where you want to go
- what type of ticket you want
- when you want to leave
- if/when you want to return

B PRACTISE Sit back-to-back with a partner. Act out a telephone call to buy a ticket. Then swap roles.

C PERSONAL BEST Listen to another pair. Write down three things that they do well.

Personal Best   Write a conversation between a customer and a travel agent about a new trip.

Grammar

1 Choose the correct options to complete the questions and sentences.

1 Where _____ last night?
   a you were
   b were you
   c you was

2 Our taxi driver _____ very friendly.
   a wasn't
   b not was
   c weren't

3 She _____ work at 7.00 p.m. last night.
   a did finish
   b finishes
   c finished

4 _____ football at the weekend?
   a Did you play
   b You did play
   c You played

5 They _____ to Oslo for a meeting.
   a did fly
   b flied
   c flew

6 We had a map, so we _____ lost .
   a didn't get
   b didn't got
   c not got

7 _____ a restaurant in your hotel?
   a There was
   b Was there
   c Were there

8 _____ two police officers in the street last night.
   a There was
   b They were
   c There were

2 Rewrite the questions and sentences in the past simple.

1 Does she play tennis with Laura?
   _____ last weekend?

2 There are two eggs in the fridge.
   _____ last night.

3 I don't have time for breakfast.
   _____ this morning.

4 I ride my bike to work.
   _____ yesterday.

5 Do you go to the gym?
   _____ last Saturday?

6 He gets on the 8.00 a.m. train.
   _____ yesterday.

3 Complete the text with the past simple form of the verbs in brackets.

Birds for friends

In many countries people give food to birds in parks or in their gardens. But Gabi Mann from Seattle in the USA has a very special relationship with the birds in her neighbourhood – they bring *her* presents!
The story ¹_____ (start) when Gabi ²_____ (be) four years old. She ³_____ (have) some food in the car and when she ⁴_____ (get out), the food fell on the ground. There ⁵_____ (be) a crow near the car and it ⁶_____ (fly) down to eat the food.
After that, Gabi ⁷_____ (not eat) all of her lunch at school. Instead she kept some and ⁸_____ (give) it to the birds on the way home. In 2013, she ⁹_____ (help) more birds and put food and water in the garden every morning. One day the crows started bringing things like buttons, rocks, small pieces of metal or plastic and even jewellery for Gabi. ¹⁰_____ they _____ (want) to say 'thank you' to her? Gabi thinks so. She collects these 'presents' and she now has more than 100. Her favourite is a metal heart. 'It shows me how much they love me,' she says.

Vocabulary

1 Put the words in the box in the correct columns.

| summer April cold field fifth autumn first flower grass hot March May mountain winter ninth October second spring warm wet |

Months	Ordinal numbers	Weather	Nature	Seasons

2 Circle the word that is different. Explain your answers.

1 artist   musician   winter   dancer
2 week   rain   month   year
3 beach   dry   sea   river
4 spring   summer   autumn   windy
5 snow   ride   sail   fly
6 foggy   sunny   sky   cloudy
7 forest   sixth   third   fourth
8 king   queen   tree   politician

3 Choose the correct options to complete the sentences.

1 The summer in India is very _____ and wet.
   a hot   b sun   c cold
2 My sister _____ the train at King's Cross Station.
   a gets on   b gets in   c gets out
3 Don't _____ your bus! It leaves in five minutes.
   a take   b miss   c get lost
4 There are lots of big trees in this _____ .
   a flower   b foggy   c forest
5 Did you _____ your ticket to New York yesterday?
   a fly   b book   c sail
6 He _____ of the car at the police station.
   a got out   b got off   c got on
7 The _____ played the piano very well.
   a musician   b athlete   c dancer
8 It was a beautiful day, so we _____ to the park.
   a walked   b watched   c worked
9 With my smartphone, I never _____ in a new city.
   a miss   b get out   c get lost
10 You can't swim in the _____ . It's very dangerous.
   a river   b field   c sky

4 Complete the sentences with the words in the box.

| ago   6.00   at (x2)   summer   in (x2) |
| Friday   last   on   yesterday   May |

1 I went to Greece _____ year on holiday.
2 Did you meet your friends on _____ ?
3 He started work _____ 7.00 this morning.
4 We usually go shopping _____ Saturday.
5 We can take the train at _____ .
6 His birthday is _____ June.
7 He started a new job two weeks _____ .
8 The first of _____ is a public holiday.
9 I played tennis with my brother _____ .
10 What did you do _____ the weekend?
11 She lived in Bogotá _____ 2016.
12 We didn't go on holiday in the _____ .

Personal Best

Lesson 7A
Name five celebrities with different jobs.

Lesson 8A
List five irregular verbs and their past simple forms.

Lesson 7A
Write where you were on two different days last week.

Lesson 8B
Describe the weather in your favourite season.

Lesson 7B
Write the birthdays of four friends or family members.

Lesson 8B
Write three sentences with *quite*, *very* and *really* and an adjective.

Lesson 7C
Write three sentences beginning *Last year ...*, *Two years ago ...* and *Yesterday ...* .

Lesson 8C
Name five things from nature you can see out of the window.

Lesson 7C
List five regular verbs and their past simple forms.

Lesson 8C
Write two sentences about your home as a child. Use *There was ...* and *There were ...* .

Lesson 7D
Describe what you did yesterday with *First*, *Then* and *After that*.

Lesson 8D
Write three sentences for buying a train ticket.

Shopping

LANGUAGE present continuous ■ clothes

9A Street style

1 Match the words in the box with the clothes in the picture.

| belt jeans jacket T-shirt hat |

1 _____ 2 _____ 3 _____ 4 _____ 5 _____

Go to Vocabulary practice: clothes, page 128

Personal Best

2 Discuss the questions in pairs.

1 What do you usually wear …
   a at home? b at work/in class? c on holiday?
2 Where do you usually buy your clothes? What's your favourite shop?
3 Do you buy second-hand clothes? Why/Why not?

3 Read the text and answer the questions.

1 Where is Sukanya from?
3 Why does she buy these clothes?
2 What type of clothes does she wear?
4 Where does she take Mark?

Fashion Diary with Mark Ashcroft

This week, I'm in Thailand with local fashion blogger Sukanya Tanasan. Sukanya only wears second-hand clothes, but she looks amazing!
'There are some great places to buy clothes in Bangkok,' she says. 'If I need a new dress, a T-shirt or shoes, I always go to the markets. You can find really cool clothes there and they're cheap too!'
Today, Sukanya takes me to the Chatuchak market in Bangkok on a shopping trip.

▶ PLAY ⬇ DOWNLOAD

4 ▶9.2 Listen and tick (✔) the things Sukanya buys.
T-shirt ☐ dress ☐ shoes ☐ hat ☐ skirt ☐

5 A ▶9.2 Complete the sentences with the words in the box. Listen again and check.

| getting buying taking eating leaving doing |

1 We're _____ the train to Chatuchak market.
2 A lot of people are _____ out here.
3 She's _____ the dress!
4 What's this man _____ ?
5 Sukanya, you aren't _____ the rice!
6 We're _____ the market now.

B Look at sentences 1–6 again and answer the questions. Then read the Grammar box.

1 What are the sentences about? *things happening now / regular events*
2 Which three letters are at the end of the main verbs? _____
3 Which verb do we use before the main verb? *be / do*

📖 **Grammar** present continuous

Things that are happening now

Positive:
I**'m going** to the market.
We**'re getting off** the bus.

Negative:
She **isn't having** a drink.
They **aren't wearing** glasses.

Questions and short answers:
Are you **working** today?
Yes, I **am**. No, I**'m not**.

Go to Grammar practice: present continuous, page 104

6 Complete the phone messages with the present continuous form of the verbs in brackets.

7 A ▶9.4 **Pronunciation:** *-ing* endings Listen and repeat. Pay attention to the /ɪŋ/ sound in **bold**.

com**ing** go**ing** do**ing** runn**ing** wait**ing** stay**ing**

B ▶9.5 Say the questions and sentences. Then listen, check and repeat.

1 Where are you going?
2 She's running for her bus.
3 I'm not doing any work.
4 Are you staying?
5 He's coming to the café.
6 We're waiting for a taxi.

Go to Communication practice: Student A page 150, Student B page 149

8 In pairs, ask and answer the question *What is/are ... doing?* about the people in the pictures.

A *What's David doing?*
B *I think he's having lunch in a restaurant.*

Jorge ● online

Hi Jorge, what ¹_____ you _____ (do)?
I ²_____ (go) to the town centre with Silvia. 11.35

Cool! I'm there too. 11.36

Do you want to have a coffee in 30 mins?
The café on Bridge Street? 11.36

👊 11.37

I ³_____ (sit) next to the window.
Silvia ⁴_____ (not/stay). She needs to
buy a new dress. Are you here? 12.05

I ⁵_____ (get) a coffee.
Do you want one? 12.10

⁶_____ you _____ (come) ?! 12.19

Sorry. My battery died. I ⁷_____ (run)
to the café now. 12.25

Too late. We ⁸_____ (wait)
for the bus home. 12.26

😔 12.26

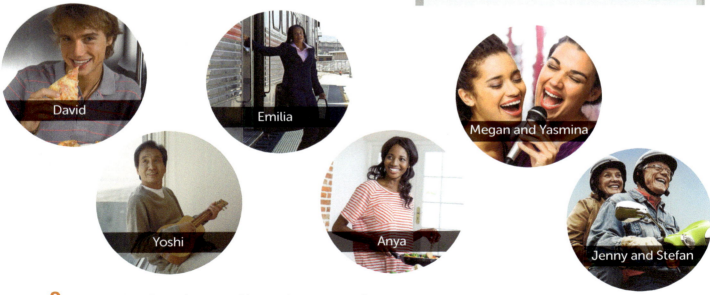

David

Emilia

Megan and Yasmina

Yoshi

Anya

Jenny and Stefan

9 In pairs, describe a classmate. Your partner guesses the person.

A *She's wearing a blue dress and she's sitting next to Leon.*
B *Is it Malika?*
A *Yes, it is!*

Personal Best Think of six people you know. Write sentences about what they're doing at the moment.

9B How do you feel?

1 Match the words in the box with pictures a–f.

angry   calm   excited   hungry   thirsty   tired

Go to Vocabulary practice: feelings, page 129

2 ▶9.7 Complete the text with four feelings from exercise 1. Listen and check.

Colours and feelings

 Colours can sometimes change how we feel. For example, orange can make us feel happy and **1**_____ . A lot of restaurants, for example McDonald's and KFC, use red because it can make us feel **2**_____ . Offices often use blue because it makes us **3**_____ . But grey isn't a popular colour for offices because it can make us feel sad or **4**_____ .

3 A Look at the picture of Ethan. How does his shirt make you feel?

B ▶9.8 Match the colours in the box with sentences 1–4. Watch or listen to the first part of *Learning Curve* and check.

orange   blue   white   black   yellow

1 Doctors often wear this colour.   _____
2 Firefighters usually wear these colours. _____ or _____
3 The police in the USA wear this colour.   _____
4 People wear this colour when they're sad. _____

Skill   identifying key points

When people speak, try to listen for the important things they say.
- We often emphasize or repeat the most important ideas.
- We sometimes give examples or more information.

4 ▶9.8 Read the Skill box. Then watch or listen again. Tick (✔) the **two** key points Ethan talks about.

a Colours can change how we feel. ☐
b Colours are important in festivals all around the world. ☐
c Orange is a popular colour for clothes. ☐
d Workers sometimes wear uniforms of the same colour. ☐

5 Discuss the questions in pairs.

1 Do you wear a uniform for work?
2 Did you wear a uniform at school?
3 What colours are/were the uniforms?
4 How do/did they make you feel?

6 ▶ 9.9 Watch or listen to the rest of the show. Match the feelings in the box with the people.

bored   excited   scared   hungry   thirsty

 Udo

 Akiko

 Penny

 Bob

1 _____   2 _____   3 _____   4 _____ and _____

7 ▶ 9.9 Watch or listen again. Choose the correct options to complete the key points.

1 Udo _____ .
  a makes his own clothes   b buys expensive clothes   c only wears bright colours
2 Akiko _____ .
  a doesn't like *Learning Curve*   b doesn't like Ethan's shirt   c is late for class
3 Bob _____ .
  a loves the colour yellow   b wears a uniform for work   c wants to eat something

8 Ask and answer the questions in the boxes.

What are you wearing today?   What colours are the clothes?   How do they make you feel?

9 ▶ 9.10 Read the two extracts. Can you understand them without the missing words? Listen and write the missing words.

1 _____ Penny, what are people wearing today? Do you see a lot of colours on the streets of New York?

2 _____ , people are leaving work at the moment. Let's see what they're wearing.

🧩 **Listening builder**   filler words

When people speak, they often say short words while they are thinking of what to say. You can ignore these words – they don't really mean anything.
So, what are you, **er**, wearing today?
Well, I'm wearing blue jeans and, **um**, this red T-shirt.

10 ▶ 9.11 Read the Listening builder. Then listen to the description of the photo. Tick (✔) the sentences the speaker says.

1 a This photo is of a young girl in a school. ☐
  b In this photo, there's a young girl at school. ☐
  c The photo shows a young girl in school. ☐
2 a And she's wearing a grey uniform and glasses. ☐
  b And she has a long grey uniform and glasses. ☐
  c And she's wearing a uniform and some glasses. ☐
3 a She's standing near the teacher's desk. ☐
  b In the class, there aren't any teachers. ☐
  c I think she's waiting for the teacher. ☐

11 Discuss the questions in pairs.

1 What are your favourite colours?   3 Which colours don't you like?
2 How do they make you feel?   4 How do they make you feel?

Personal Best   Describe the colours in the rooms in your house and say how they make you feel.

9C Love it or hate it?

1 Complete phrases 1–5 with the words in the box.

buy   pay   shop   sell   try on

1 _____ shoes
2 _____ by credit card
3 _____ fruit
4 _____ online
5 _____ a new car

Go to Vocabulary practice: shopping, page 130

2 Do the questionnaire in pairs. Write down your partner's answers. Then go to page 147 and look at the results.

Shopping – do you love it or hate it?

1 How often do you go to a shopping centre?
a Never! I hate shopping centres.
b I only go when I need some new clothes.
c I go there every week. I love it!

2 Do you spend a lot of money on clothes and shoes?
a No, I don't. I usually buy second-hand clothes.
b When I have a special occasion – once or twice a year.
c Yes, I do. Clothes are very important to me.

3 How often do you shop online?
a Not often. Maybe once a year.
b A few times a month.
c Very often. Three or four times a week.

4 How do you feel if you need to buy a present for someone?
a Bored. I prefer to give cash as a present.
b Happy. I can find something in a local shop.
c Really excited! I can go shopping all day on Saturday!

5 How do you usually pay when you go shopping?
a I pay with cash. I never spend money that I don't have.
b I sometimes pay with cash and sometimes by card.
c I usually pay by credit card.

3 A Complete the questions and sentences from the questionnaire with the words in the box.

how   every   times   twice   often   once

1 How _____ do you go to a shopping centre?
2 I go there _____ week.
3 Once or _____ a year.
4 _____ often do you shop online?
5 Maybe _____ a year.
6 Three or four _____ a week.

B Which tense do we use to talk about the frequency of events? *present simple / present continuous* Read the Grammar box.

Grammar ***how often* + expressions of frequency**

***How often* do you go shopping?**

| I go shopping | ***once a*** *twice a* **three/four times a** **every** | **day/week/month/year.** |

Go to Grammar practice: *how often* + expressions of frequency, page 104

4 A ▶9.14 **Pronunciation:** sentence stress Listen and repeat the expressions of frequency. Pay attention to the <u>underlined</u> stressed words.

1 <u>once</u> a <u>day</u>
2 <u>twice</u> a <u>year</u>
3 <u>three</u> <u>times</u> a <u>month</u>
4 <u>every</u> <u>day</u> and <u>every</u> <u>night</u>

B ▶9.15 Say the sentences. Pay attention to the sentence stress. Listen, check and repeat.

1 I call my girlfriend twice a day.
2 We go to the cinema every month.
3 They shop online three times a week.
4 My grandparents visit every year.

Go to Communication practice: Student A page 141, Student B page 149

5 A Write the questions.

1 How often / you buy someone a present?
_____
_____
_____

4 How often / it snow in your town?
_____
_____
_____

2 How often / your teacher give homework?
_____
_____
_____

5 How often / you go to bed after midnight?
_____
_____
_____

3 How often / you wash your hair?
_____
_____
_____

6 How often / you pay by credit card?
_____
_____
_____

B In pairs, ask and answer the questions.

A *How often do you buy someone a present?*
B *I buy someone a present once or twice a month. How about you?*

6 A Write three true sentences and three false sentences about you with expressions of frequency.
B Read your sentences to your partner. Guess if they are true or false.

A *I go to Singapore twice a year.*
B *I think that's false.*
A *No, it's true! My sister lives there.*

9D Garage sale

1 A What do you do with things you don't use any more?

a Throw them away.
b Take them to a second-hand shop.
c Sell them online.
d Have a garage sale.

B Discuss the questions in pairs.

1 How often do you buy second-hand things?
2 What type of second-hand things do you buy?
3 Do people have garage sales in your country?
4 Do you think they're a good idea? Why/Why not?

2 A Read the email quickly. What relationship is the writer to Patrick?

B Read the email again. Match the names in the box with the people in the picture.

Bill Sandra Evie Eddie

Hi Patrick,

How are you?

a We had a garage sale yesterday. It was at our house and we sold some old clothes, books and other things.

b Here's a photo. The man on the right is our friend, Bill. He's looking at our old things. His wife Sandra is on the left, and the girl in the middle is their daughter, Evie. She's trying on my old hat. There's an old skateboard at the bottom of the photo – I think it's your dad's. The man at the top of the picture is our neighbour, Eddie. He's looking at a pair of Grandpa's old trousers!

c We made about £100! We bought some new chairs for the garden with the money.

Email me soon with your news.

Grandma

3 A Match paragraphs a–c with the parts of the email 1–3.

1 description of photo _____
2 what happened after _____
3 introduction _____

B What tenses are the verbs in paragraphs a–c? Read the Skill box.

Skill | describing a photo

When we describe a photo, we:
- explain who the people are: *The man on the right is our friend, Bill.*
- use the present continuous to say what they are doing: *She's trying on my old hat.*
- use *there is/are* to say what things are in the picture: *There's an old skateboard ...*

4 Complete Patrick's reply with the correct form of the verbs in brackets.

Dear Grandma,

I'm very well, thanks. That's great about the garage sale!

I ¹_____ (go) to Bristol last Saturday with some friends. We ²_____ (take) the train in the morning and we ³_____ (explore) the city.

Here's a photo. The girl on the left is Sara and the girl in the middle is Lisa. They ⁴_____ (be) my classmates from university. They ⁵_____ (try) to find the Clifton Suspension Bridge on the map. Lisa's boyfriend, Shaun, is on the right. He ⁶_____ (take) a photo of some street art.

It was a fun day out, but we ⁷_____ (be) all really tired when we ⁸_____ (get) home!

Love Patrick x

5 Match the halves to make sentences. Check your answers in the emails.

1 The man on	a the left is Sara.
2 The girl in	b the middle is their daughter, Evie.
3 There's an old skateboard at	c the right is our friend, Bill.
4 The man at	d the top of the picture is our neighbour, Eddie.
5 The girl on	e the bottom of the photo.

Text builder   describing position

▶ *on the right*	▲ *at the top*	✕ *in the middle*
◀ *on the left*	▼ *at the bottom*	◥ *in the corner*

---

6 A Read the Text builder. Then write sentences.

1 that / my brother / right   _That's my brother on the right._
2 my friend Casey / middle   _____
3 there / a cat / corner   _____
4 that / my cousin / top   _____
5 there / more people / left   _____

B In pairs, take a photo of some of your classmates. Describe the photo using phrases from the Text builder.

That's Nacho on the left and Lourdes is on the right. There's a blue bag in the corner. It's Nacho's bag.

7 A PREPARE Choose one of the photos. Imagine that you took it. Make notes to answer the questions.

1 When and where did you take the photo?
2 Who are the people in the photo?
3 What are they doing?
4 What happened after you took the photo?

B PRACTISE Write an email. Introduce the photo, describe it and say what happened after you took it.

C PERSONAL BEST Swap emails with your partner and read it. Check the tenses of the verbs and prepositions for describing position. Can you improve anything?

Personal Best   Write an email describing one of your own photos.

Time out

LANGUAGE present continuous for future plans ■ free-time activities

10A What are you doing at the weekend?

1 A Look at the poster for a music festival. Discuss the questions in pairs.

1 Do you know this music festival?
2 Where and when is the festival?
3 Do you like music festivals? Why/Why not?
4 What can you see in the pictures?

B Complete the text with the words in the box.

> visit go watch have stay

COACHELLA
Music and Arts
Festival

Win tickets for an incredible Coachella experience

Call **08081 570000** and tell us why you want to go.

1 _____ to all the concerts
2 _____ in a luxury tent
3 _____ the art area and see amazing sculptures
4 _____ films at night
5 _____ a good time!

April 14–16
Coachella Valley, California

Personal Best

Go to Vocabulary practice: free-time activities, page 131

2 ▶ 10.2 Read and listen to the conversation between two friends. Where is Alex going this weekend?

Alex Guess what I'm doing this weekend.
Dan I don't know. Are you visiting your family again?
Alex No, I'm not. I'm going to a music festival – Coachella! I won tickets in a competition.
Dan Coachella? No way! Which bands are playing?
Alex Radiohead are playing on Friday and Lady Gaga on Saturday.
Dan That's amazing. Are you going on your own?
Alex No, the prize was for two tickets.
Dan Two tickets? You know, I'm not doing anything this weekend …
Alex Sorry, Dan. I'm going with my mother.
Dan Your mother?
Alex Yeah, she loves Lady Gaga. We're driving there tonight and then we're staying in a tent all weekend!
Dan Well, have a good time. Tell me all about it on Monday, OK?

3 Are the sentences true (T) or false (F)? Check your answers in the conversation.

1 Dan's going to Coachella with Alex. _____
2 Lady Gaga's playing on Saturday. _____
3 They're driving to the festival tonight. _____
4 They're staying in a hotel all weekend. _____

4 **A** Look at the sentences in exercise 3 again. Answer the questions.

1 Which tense are the verbs? *present simple / past simple / present continuous*
2 When do the actions happen? *in the past / now / in the future*

B Find more examples of this tense in the conversation in exercise 2. Then read the Grammar box.

> 📖 **Grammar** **present continuous for future plans**
>
> **Positive:**
> I'**m going** to a music festival this weekend.
> We'**re visiting** a museum tomorrow.
>
> **Negative:**
> Sue **isn't going** to the concert tonight.
> They **aren't staying** in a hotel.
>
> **Questions and short answers:**
> **Are** you **having** a party in the summer?
> Yes, I **am**. No, I'**m not**.

Go to Grammar practice: present continuous for future plans, page 105

5 **A** ▶10.5 **Pronunciation:** sentence stress Listen and repeat the questions and answers from the conversation in exercise 2. Pay attention to the <u>underlined</u> stressed words.

1 Are you <u>visiting</u> your <u>family</u>?   <u>No</u>, I'm <u>not</u>.
2 <u>Which</u> <u>bands</u> are <u>playing</u>?   <u>Radiohead</u> are <u>playing</u> on <u>Friday</u>.

B ▶10.6 Match the questions with answers a–c. Ask and answer the questions in pairs with the correct stress. Listen, check and repeat.

1 What are you doing this weekend?   a I'm taking the bus.
2 How are you getting there?   b Yes, I am.
3 Are you staying with friends?   c I'm going to the beach.

6 Look at Rosie's diary on her smartphone. In pairs, ask and answer the question *What's she doing ...?* with the times in the box.

> ~~this morning~~   on Friday   tomorrow   at the weekend
> the day after tomorrow   this evening

A *What's she doing this morning?*
B *She's having coffee with Kate.*

Go to Communication practice:
Student A page 141, Student B page 149

7 **A** ▶10.7 Use the words to write questions in the present continuous. Listen to the conversation and check.

1 What / you / do / at the weekend?
_____

2 Who / you / go / with?
_____

3 How / you / get / there?
_____

4 When / you / leave?
_____

5 Where / you / stay?
_____

B ▶10.7 Listen again and write Cheryl's answers to the questions.

8 **A** Make notes about your plans for the weekend. They can be real or imaginary.

B In pairs, ask and answer the questions in exercise 7 about your plans.

A *What are you doing at the weekend?*   **B** *I'm having a barbecue with my friends.*

< May	Q +
Tuesday 6 (today)	
11:00	Coffee with Kate
19:30	Cinema with Malika
Wednesday 7	
11.15	Meet Sandra
Thursday 8	
14:00	Picasso exhibition
Friday 9	
20:00	My party!
Saturday 10	
10:30	Visit Mum and Dad
📅 View Today	✉ Inbox (4)

Personal Best   Write a paragraph about your 'perfect' weekend.

10B What's on?

1 ▶ 10.8 Listen and match the words in the box with the types of music and film.

> classical   science-fiction   action   jazz   electronic   romance

1 _____   2 _____   3 _____   4 _____   5 _____   6 _____

Go to Vocabulary practice: types of music and film, page 132

2 Look at the webpage on page 89. What type of website is it? Do you use websites like this?

> **Skill** scanning for information
>
> 'Scanning' means looking quickly at a text to find specific information.
> - Underline the key word(s) in the question.
> - Look for the word(s) in the text quickly. Use your finger to help you.
> - When you find the word, read the information to answer the question.

3 **A** Read the Skill box. Then read questions 1–4 and scan the text for the answers. The key words are underlined.

1 What time does the concert start? _____
2 Where is the art exhibition? _____
3 How much is a cinema ticket for children? _____
4 Which event is free to enter? _____

B Read questions 1–4 and underline the key words. Then scan the text for the answers.

1 What's the name of the theatre in the city? _____
2 How old do you need to be to try speed dating? _____
3 Which event costs less if you buy tickets online? _____
4 Who's playing electronic music tonight? _____

4 Look at the text and discuss the questions in pairs.

1 Which events do you want to go to? Why?
2 Which events aren't you interested in? Why?

5 Complete the sentences from the text with the correct words.

1 Don't _____ it!
2 _____ to our Speed Dating night!
3 _____ all night.
4 _____ very scared!

> **Text builder** the imperative
>
> We use the imperative to give instructions.
> **Book** early!   **Open** the window!   **Don't be** late!   **Don't forget** about the party!

6 Read the Text builder. Then complete the sentences with the positive or negative imperative of the verbs in the box.

> call   listen   talk   sit   open   be

1 _____ down, please. I can't see the film.
2 The concert starts at 7.45, so _____ late.
3 _____ to this great song. I love it!
4 _____ the window, please. It's very hot.
5 Please _____ in the library. I'm trying to read.
6 _____ me today because I'm working.

7 Discuss the questions in pairs.

1 What's your favourite type of music?
2 When do you listen to music?
3 How often do you go to concerts/nightclubs?
4 What type of films do you like?
5 What was the last film you saw?
6 How often do you go to the cinema?

What's On

Events in your area: Saturday 9 June   Sort by: Date ⬍

Visitors
Science-fiction adventure. When aliens arrive on Earth, do they want to help people – or start a war?
ABC Cinema, 6.30 p.m. 9.00 p.m. 11.30 p.m.
Tickets £10. Under-16s: £8

🎟 Buy Tickets

Anderson .Paak in concert
Anderson .Paak brings his mix of jazz, hip-hop and rock to the city. Don't miss it!
Royal Arena, 8.00 p.m.
Tickets £17.50

🎟 Sold Out

Romeo and Juliet
William Shakespeare's great love story. A boy and a girl find love on the streets of Verona.
King's Theatre, 7.15 p.m.
Tickets £18.00

🎟 Sold Out

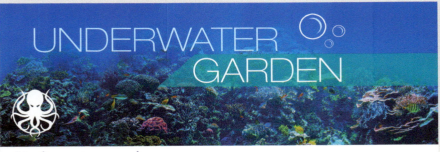

Underwater garden
Dance all night as DJ Octopus plays the latest in electronic music from around the world.
Club Infinity, 10.00 p.m.–late   **Entry £8.00 (Over-18s only)**

🎟 Buy Tickets

Hot Potato
Enjoy an evening of comedy with Sally Quentin. 'Really funny' *The Daily Times*. Book online and save £5.
Comedy Club, 7.00 p.m.
Tickets £15 on the door

🎟 Buy Tickets

Looking for love?
Are you single? Do you want to find that special person? Come to our Speed Dating night – the fun way to meet new people!
Union Café, 6.30 p.m.
Admission £15. Minimum age 21

🎟 Buy Tickets

Book reading with Joe Arnott
Joe Arnott reads from his new horror story, *Play With Fire*. Be scared, be very scared!
Forest Hill Library, 8.00 p.m.
Admission free. Over-16s only.

🎟 Reserve

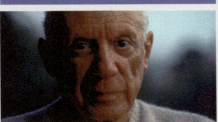

Picasso's portraits
Exhibition of paintings and sculptures from one of the most popular artists of the twentieth century.
Trinidad Gallery
Tickets £12.50

🎟 Buy Tickets

10C Royal hobbies

1 Complete the sports and games with the verbs *go*, *play* and *do*.

1 _____ tennis   2 _____ karate   3 _____ running   4 _____ rock climbing   5 _____ videogames   6 _____ yoga

Personal Best

Go to Vocabulary practice: sports and games, page 133

2 In pairs, ask and answer the question *Do you ...?* with the correct verbs and the sports and games in the box.

A *Do you go cycling?*   **B** *Yes, I do. I usually go cycling once a week.*

> cycling   swimming   football   Pilates   gymnastics   basketball   chess   karate   skiing

3 A Who are the people in the picture? Read the text and check. What do you know about them?

B ▶ 10.11 Guess which three activities in exercise 1 the people do. Listen to the interview and check.

4 A ▶ 10.11 Complete the interviewer's questions with the words in the box. Listen again and check.

> was   where   how   does   is   what

1 _____ does he relax?
2 _____ is his favourite game?
3 _____ did she go to university?
4 _____ she good at sports?
5 _____ William do lots of exercise too?
6 _____ he training for a marathon now?

B Look at questions 1–6 again.

1 Which questions do you answer with *yes* or *no*? ____ ____ ____
2 Which questions do you answer with specific information? ____ ____ ____

5 A Match the tenses in the box with the questions in 4A.

> past simple   present continuous   present simple (x2)   present simple of *be*   past simple of *be*

1 _____   2 _____   3 _____   4 _____   5 _____   6 _____

B Match the words in the box with the parts of the question 1–4. Then read the Grammar box.

> subject   question word   main verb   auxiliary verb

1 What _____   2 do _____   3 they _____   4 do _____ in their free time?

7.00 p.m.

Relaxing with
the Royals

What do Prince Harry, Prince William and his wife Kate, the Duchess of Cambridge, do in their free time? Royal expert Jenny Brown joins us to talk about how the young royals relax.

📖 Grammar   question review

Most verbs: (question word) + auxiliary verb + subject + main verb:

Where do you live?   *What are you doing?*   *When did they arrive?*
Does Carla play tennis?   *Is he watching TV?*   *Did you go running yesterday?*

The verb *be*: (question word) + *be* + subject:

How old are you?   *Where was Antonio yesterday?*
Is the milk in the fridge? *Were you worried about the exam?*

Go to Grammar practice: question review, page 105

6 A ▶ 10.14 **Pronunciation:** Intonation in questions Listen and repeat the questions.
Pay attention to the intonation that goes up (↗) or down (↘).

questions with question words	*yes/no* questions
1 Which films do you like? ↘	3 Is she from Japan? ↗
2 Where are they going? ↘	4 Did you stay in a hotel? ↗

B ▶ 10.15 Say the questions with the correct intonation. Listen, check and repeat.
Then ask and answer the questions in pairs.

1 What are you doing tonight?
2 Did you cook dinner yesterday?
3 Where were you at 7.00 this morning?
4 How often do you take the bus?
5 Is it raining at the moment?
6 Does our teacher like pop music?

Go to Communication practice: Student A page 141, Student B page 150

7 A ▶ 10.16 Order the words to make questions 1–6. Listen and check.

B ▶ 10.16 In pairs, ask and answer the questions. Listen again and check.

Estonian fashion model Carmen Kass plays chess.

1 start / did / when / she
_____ ?

2 she / how / did / learn
_____ ?

American singer Elvis Presley did karate.

3 karate / at / was / good / he
_____ ?

4 where / do / did / it / he
_____ ?

American actor Lucy Liu goes rock climbing.

5 go / how / rock climbing / she / does / often
_____ ?

6 dangerous / is / it
_____ ?

---

8 Choose a sport or game that you do. In pairs, ask and answer the questions in the boxes.

> What's your hobby?   When did you start?   Where do you do it?   How often do you do it?
>
> Are you doing it this weekend?   Is it difficult?   Is it expensive?
>
> How did you learn?   Who do you do it with?   What do you need to do it?

Learning Curve

10D Where are we going now?

a

b

1 Look at the pictures and answer the questions.

1 Which tourist attractions can you see?
2 Which countries are they in?
3 Do you want to visit them? Why/Why not?
4 What tourist attractions are there in your town/city?

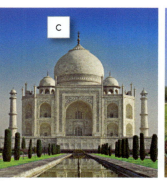

c

d

e

f

2 A ▶ 10.17 Watch or listen to the first part of *Learning Curve*. Where is Ethan? Who does he meet?

B ▶ 10.17 Choose the correct options to complete the sentences. Watch or listen again and check.

1 Flushing Meadows is famous for its *football stadium / tennis stadium*.
2 There were two World's Fairs in the park – in 1939 and in *1964 / 1974*.
3 There is a *science museum / design museum* in the park.
4 Ethan, Penny and Taylor are meeting Marc in *half an hour / an hour*.
5 Marc and Taylor *know / don't know* each other.

3 ▶ 10.18 Listen and complete the questions in the conversation.

> **Taylor** So what time [1]_____ the Hall of Science _____?
> **Ethan** It opens at 10.00 a.m.
> **Penny** What [2]_____ _____ to do if it rains?
> **Ethan** Well, we can stay inside and look at exhibits all day.
> **Penny** OK. Sounds good. When [3]_____ it _____?
> **Ethan** 6.00 p.m.
> **Taylor** OK, great. So, what [4]_____ we _____ now?
> **Ethan** We're meeting our friend Marc from *Learning Curve*, at the Information Desk.

🧩 **Conversation builder**   **asking about a tourist attraction**

What time does it open/close?   *Is there a café/restaurant/gift shop?*
Which days is it open?   *What is there to do if it rains?*
How do you get there?   *Are there any special events?*

4 A Read the Conversation builder. Then look at the information about a tourist attraction on page 93. Ask and answer questions in pairs.

A *What time does it open?*   **B** *It opens at 9.30 a.m.*

B Do you want to visit this attraction? Why/Why not?

Fun days out **Legoland** > Plan your trip   Week: 13–19 September 📅

Monday	Tuesday	Wednesday	Thursday	Friday	Saturday	Sunday
● 9.30 a.m. – 5.00 p.m. (£30)				● 9.30 a.m. – 6.00 p.m. (£35)			● Closed

Weather: Most attractions are outside. Umbrellas are available from the gift shop. Inside attractions include: LEGO 4D Movie Theatre, Imagination Centre and the Exploratorium workshops.

Food & drink: City Walk Pizza and Pasta, Hill Top Café and many more.

Getting there:
By car: Legoland is on the B3022 road (parking available).
By bus: Take the number 200 bus from Windsor Theatre Royal.

31 December: Kids' New Year's Eve firework show

5 A ▶10.19 Watch or listen to the second part of the show. How many exhibits do Penny, Marc, Ethan and Taylor see in the Hall of Science?

B ▶10.19 Are the sentences true (T) or false (F)? Watch or listen again and check.

1 Tickets for the Hall of Science cost $15. _____
2 There are almost 450 exhibits. _____
3 Marc and Ethan buy tickets for a 3D film. _____
4 Taylor doesn't like flying. _____
5 Taylor wants a flying car. _____
6 They decide to eat pizza. _____

Penny   Ethan   Marc   Taylor

6 ▶10.20 Match the sentences with the responses. Listen, check and repeat the responses.

1 It costs $15, but we paid for you.
2 What about *Journey into Space*? It's a 3D film.
3 We're hungry and we're eating a very large pizza.

a OK. Sounds good.
b Oh really? Thanks!
c That sounds interesting.

🔧 **Skill**   **showing interest**

When people speak to you, it's important to show that you're listening.
• Use expressions: *Oh really? That sounds good. Great.*
• Use intonation to sound interested.

7 A ▶10.21 Read the Skill box. Then listen to conversations 1–4. Which response sounds more interested: *a* or *b*?

1 I'm visiting my family this weekend. _____
2 My sister goes rock climbing every week. _____
3 There's a new comedy at the cinema. _____
4 We went to the beach yesterday. _____

B ▶10.22 Listen and repeat the interested responses.

Go to Communication practice: Students A and B, page 150

8 A PREPARE In pairs, invent a tourist attraction and write information about it. Include:

• the days and times it is open
• the price of tickets
• what you can do
• how to get there
• shops and restaurants
• special events

B PRACTISE Swap your information with another pair. Then ask and answer questions about the tourist attraction. Remember to show you're interested.

A *What time does the museum open?*   B *It opens at 9.30 a.m.*   A *OK, great.*

C PERSONAL BEST Listen to the other pair. Do they ask questions well? Do they show interest?

Personal Best   Write about a tourist attraction in your town/city.

Grammar

1 Tick (✔) the correct sentences.

1 a I can't talk now. I'm doing my homework. ☐
  b I can't talk now. I do my homework. ☐
  c I can't talk now. I did my homework. ☐

2 a They not working at the moment. ☐
  b They aren't working at the moment. ☐
  c They don't working at the moment. ☐

3 a What often do you go to the gym? ☐
  b How often do you go to the gym? ☐
  c How much often do you go to the gym? ☐

4 a I see my brother three times at year. ☐
  b I see my brother three times for year. ☐
  c I see my brother three times a year. ☐

5 a What are you doing tomorrow? ☐
  b What do you do tomorrow? ☐
  c What you are doing tomorrow? ☐

6 a He not is coming to the party tonight. ☐
  b He isn't coming to the party tonight. ☐
  c He doesn't come to the party tonight. ☐

7 a What time did the train leave? ☐
  b What time the train did leave? ☐
  c What time left the train? ☐

8 a They were at work yesterday? ☐
  b Did they be at work yesterday? ☐
  c Were they at work yesterday? ☐

2 Complete the questions and sentences with the correct form of the verbs in the box.

| cost finish spend go have meet |
| not be not study can buy wear |

1 How often _____ you _____ a shower?

2 Carlos _____ some new boots today. Look – they're really nice.

3 What time _____ you _____ work last night?

4 We _____ shopping in London next Tuesday.

5 How much _____ your new coat _____ ? Was it expensive?

6 She's in the library, but she _____ . She's texting a friend.

7 _____ you _____ your friends next weekend?

8 He _____ at work yesterday. I think he was ill.

9 Where _____ I _____ some good shoes?

10 How much money _____ you _____ on clothes every month?

3 Complete the text with the correct form of the verbs in brackets.

The Kinderkook Café

The Kinderkook Café in Amsterdam is a café with a difference – the chefs and waiters are all children! Parents take their children to the café in the afternoon and the children cook a meal. Then, in the evening, the parents return to eat it. Matt Baker talked to one of the parents, Sonja Kroes.

Matt   When [1]_____ the café _____ (start)?

Sonja   It started in 1981. It's very popular.

Matt   What [2]_____ the children _____ (cook)?

Sonja   They cook pasta, curry, pizza and lots more. The food is healthy and delicious.

Matt   How often [3]_____ you _____ (come) here with your daughter?

Sonja   We come once a month. Lotte loves it!

Matt   [4]_____ she _____ (work) here today?

Sonja   Yes, she is. She [5]_____ (make) a cake. Look, she's over there. She [6]_____ (wear) a pink jumper. And her friend, Stijn, is helping her. They [7]_____ (have) a good time!

Matt   [8]_____ you _____ (eat) here tonight?

Sonja   Yes, I am. I [9]_____ (come) with my husband and my parents. It was Lotte's birthday yesterday, and she wanted to have a small party here with the family.

Matt   That's nice. How old [10]_____ (be) she?

Sonja   She's seven.

Vocabulary

1 Put the words in the box in the correct columns.

| volleyball a museum videogames an art gallery |
| a suit shopping cycling gymnastics karate |
| trousers walking tennis yoga my family a belt |

go	do	visit	wear	play

2 Circle the word that is different. Explain your answers.

1	angry	happy	hockey	thirsty
2	skirt	beach	jacket	dress
3	festival	concert	suit	party
4	tent	pay	spend	buy
5	pop	rock	jazz	coat
6	socks	boots	shoes	trousers
7	museum	art gallery	jumper	department store
8	money	comedy	romance	drama

3 Choose the correct options to complete the sentences.

1 Can I try _____ this shirt, please?
   a in   **b** off   **c** on

2 That shop _____ really nice T-shirts.
   a sells   **b** spends   **c** pays

3 Let's stay _____ home tonight. I'm really tired.
   a in   **b** at   **c** on

4 Do you want to _____ a video?
   a go   **b** look   **c** watch

5 I don't have any money. Can I pay _____ card?
   a with   **b** by   **c** for

6 I usually shop _____ . I don't have time to go to the supermarket.
   a online   **b** by card   **c** by cash

7 We're _____ a barbecue at the weekend. Would you like to come?
   a having   **b** staying   **c** spending

8 We don't accept credit cards here. Can you pay with _____ , please?
   a chess   **b** cash   **c** calm

4 Complete the conversation with the words in the box.

> hungry excited time scared
> horror bored happy tired

Bella What did you do last night, Ruby?
Ruby Tim and I went to the cinema. We watched that new [1]_____ film, *Black Night*.
Bella Were you [2]_____ ?
Ruby No, we were [3]_____ . It wasn't very good.
Bella That's a pity. Did you do anything after the film?
Ruby We were really [4]_____ , so we went to a restaurant.
Bella How was the food?
Ruby It was excellent, so we were [5]_____ ! What about you? What did you do?
Bella We went to a concert – the Foo Fighters. They're Nick's favourite band. He was very [6]_____ when he got tickets.
Ruby Did you have a good [7]_____ ?
Bella Yes, it was great. The concert finished at 1.00 in the morning, so I'm really [8]_____ today!

Personal Best

Lesson 9A Name five types of clothes.

Lesson 10A Name three activities a tourist can do in your town or city.

Lesson 9A Write what three friends or family members are doing now.

Lesson 10A Write about your plans for two days next week. Use the present continuous.

Lesson 9B Name three positive feelings.

Lesson 10B Write three instructions using the imperative.

Lesson 9C Write a sentence about shopping.

Lesson 10C Name six sports or games. Use the verbs *go, play* and *do*.

Lesson 9C Write three questions with *How often …?* Then answer the questions.

Lesson 10C Write questions with *What, When* and *Where* in three different tenses.

Lesson 9D Describe a photo on your phone or in a magazine.

Lesson 10D Write three questions to ask about a tourist attraction.

6A there is/are

We use *there's* (*there is*) + *a/an* with singular nouns to say that something exists.

There's a beautiful park near my house.
There's an umbrella on the table.

We use *there are* with plural nouns to say that something exists.

There are five hotels in my city.
There are six people on the bus.

We often use *some* in positive sentences with plural nouns. We use *any* in negative sentences and questions with plural nouns.

There are some good cafés in the town centre.
There aren't any museums.
Are there any hotels near here?

▶ 6.2	Singular	Plural
+	**There's** a school. **There's** an airport.	**There are some** schools. **There are** two airports.
–	**There isn't** a cinema.	**There aren't any** cinemas.
?	**Is there** a restaurant?	**Are there any** restaurants?
Y/N	Yes, **there is**. / No, **there isn't**.	Yes, **there are**. / No, **there aren't**.

6C Prepositions of place

We use prepositions of place to say where an object or person is.

There's a table next to the bed.   *Your keys are behind the sofa.*
My brother is in the kitchen.   *Simon is next to Amy.*

▶ 6.9	Prepositions of place

 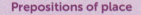         

on — The phone is **on** the table.
next to — The chair is **next to** the table.
in — The phone is **in** the bag.
in front of — The table is **in front of** the chair.
above — The shelves are **above** the table.
between — The chair is **between** the window and the table.
under — The bag is **under** the table.
behind — The lamp is **behind** the sofa.

1 Complete the sentences with the correct forms of *there is/are*.

1 _____ a great museum in town.
2 _____ a school near your house?
3 I'm sorry, but _____ a chemist near here.
4 _____ some cheap hotels near the train station.
5 _____ any parks, so children play in the street.
6 _____ any good restaurants at the shopping centre?

2 Complete the sentences with *a/an, some* or *any*.

1 There aren't _____ supermarkets in this area.
2 There's _____ good hospital near here.
3 There are _____ police officers in the street.
4 There isn't _____ Italian restaurant in our village.
5 Are there _____ pens in your bag?
6 Is there _____ police station near here?

◀ Go back to page 51

1 Look at the picture. Write sentences saying where the things are with prepositions of place.

1 fridge / cooker
_____
2 shelves / bed
_____
3 cat / table
_____
4 laptop / desk
_____
5 window / sofa
_____
6 table / sofa
_____

◀ Go back to page 55

7A   Past simple: *be*

We use the past simple of the verb *be* to talk about situations in the past.

Marilyn Monroe was an actor. She was American.

The positive past simple forms of the verb *be* are *was* and *were*.

I was in New York yesterday. The people were very friendly.

The negative past simple forms of the verb *be* are *wasn't* (*was not*) and *weren't* (*were not*).

I wasn't at home last night.
The Beatles weren't from Manchester.

We form questions with *was/were* + subject.

Was the teacher late for class?
Were you cold at work today?

▶ 7.2	I / he / she / it	you / we / they
+	I **was** happy.	They **were** singers.
–	It **wasn't** a good film.	We **weren't** at home yesterday.
?	**Was** she at school?	**Were** they Mexican?
Y/N	Yes, she **was**. / No, she **wasn't**.	Yes, they **were**. / No, they **weren't**.

1 Choose the correct words to complete the sentences.

1 My father *was / were* an artist.
2 Enrique and Javier *wasn't / weren't* at work on Monday.
3 How *was / were* your holiday?
4 This book *wasn't / weren't* very interesting.
5 My grandparents *was / were* both musicians.
6 What *was / were* the answer to this question?
7 *Were / Was* you and your sister at home yesterday?
8 We *wasn't / weren't* happy with our exam results.

2 Complete the conversations with the correct form of *was* or *were*.

1 A _____ you at home yesterday?
   B No, I _____ . I _____ at the hospital.
2 A _____ the film good?
   B Yes, it _____ . The actors _____ amazing.
3 A _____ your parents teachers?
   B No, they _____ . They _____ writers.
4 A _____ Akira Kurosawa a photographer?
   B No, he _____ . He _____ a film director.
5 A _____ you late for school today?
   B Yes, I _____ . I _____ 30 minutes late.
6 A _____ you and Nico at the same school?
   B Yes, we _____ , but we _____ in the same class.

◀ Go back to page 61

7C   Past simple: regular verbs

We use the past simple to talk about completed actions in the past. We usually add *-ed* to the infinitive to form the past simple of regular verbs.

cook ⇨ *cooked*   *I cooked pasta yesterday.*

Spelling rules for regular positive past simple *verbs*
We usually add *-ed* to the infinitive.
cook ⇨ *cooked*
When a verb ends in *-e*, we add *-d*.
dance ⇨ *danced*
When a verb ends in consonant + *y*, we change the *y* to *i* and then we add *-ed*.
study ⇨ *studied*
When a verb ends in vowel + consonant, we usually double the consonant and add *-ed*.
stop ⇨ *stopped*

We form the negative with *didn't* (*did not*) + infinitive.

I didn't want coffee for breakfast.   *My parents didn't like the food.*

We form questions with *did* + subject + infinitive.

Did she play the piano yesterday?   *Did your brother live in Canada?*

▶ 7.12	I / you / he / she / it / we / they
+	He **worked** in London.
–	They **didn't live** in this house.
?	**Did** you **study** Spanish at university?
Y/N	Yes, I **did**. / No, I **didn't**.

1 Rewrite the sentences and questions in the past simple.

1 My grandfather lives in this street.
   _____
2 I cook paella for dinner.
   _____
3 She doesn't cycle home.
   _____
4 The train doesn't stop in Paris.
   _____
5 Liam studies Science at university.
   _____
6 Does she dance with her friends?
   _____
7 Do they live in Ecuador?
   _____
8 Elise doesn't want ice cream.
   _____

◀ Go back to page 65

8A Past simple: irregular verbs

A lot of common verbs have an irregular past simple form (for a full list of irregular verbs see page 151).

take ⇒ took	*I took a taxi to the airport.*
go ⇒ went	*We went to the park yesterday.*
buy ⇒ bought	*I bought a new bag.*

Only the positive forms are irregular. We form the negative with *didn't* + infinitive.

We didn't take the train.
They didn't go to the party.
My sister didn't buy coffee.

We form questions with *did* + subject + infinitive.

Did they take the train?
Did you go to the supermarket?
Did we buy any vegetables?

▶ 8.2	I / you / he / she / it / we / they
+	He **went** to university in Edinburgh.
–	She **didn't have** breakfast yesterday.
?	**Did** you **see** Carly at the party?
Y/N	Yes, I **did**. / No, I **didn't**.

1 Complete the sentences with the past simple form of the verbs in brackets.

1 They _____ to work by car. (go)
2 She _____ to Hong Kong. (fly)
3 I _____ on the 11.30 bus to Newcastle. (get)
4 Paula _____ her daughter a lot of stories. (tell)
5 Richard _____ coffee and toast for breakfast. (have)
6 Clarissa _____ 'Hi'. (say)
7 I _____ pasta for dinner. (make)
8 My mum _____ to work yesterday. (drive)

2 Complete the questions and answers with the correct form of the verbs in brackets.

1 A What time _____ her train _____ ? (leave)
  B It _____ at 8.00 p.m.
2 A _____ you _____ a dress to the party? (wear)
  B No, I _____ a dress. I _____ jeans.
3 A _____ he _____ a bus to the station? (take)
  B No, he _____ a bus. He _____ the underground.
4 A _____ you _____ well last night? (sleep)
  B No. I _____ at all!
5 A _____ you _____ a big lunch? (have)
  B No, I _____ . I _____ a sandwich.
6 A _____ you _____ to your dad yesterday? (speak)
  B No, but I _____ to my mum.

◀ Go back to page 69

8C *there was/were*

We use *there was/were* and *a/an* with singular nouns to say that something existed in the past.

There was a big school here 50 years ago.
There was an egg in the fridge yesterday.

We use *there were* with plural nouns to say that something existed in the past.

There were lots of fields here in the past.
There were two books on my desk.

We often use *some* in positive sentences with plural nouns. We use *any* in negative sentences and questions.

There were some people in the shop.
There weren't any children.
Were there any cakes in the supermarket?

▶ 8.9	Singular	Plural
+	**There was** a road. **There was** an old house.	**There were** two shops. **There were some** trees.
–	**There wasn't** a supermarket.	**There weren't any** restaurants.
?	**Was there** a school?	**Were there any** tall buildings?
Y/N	Yes, **there was**. / No, **there wasn't**.	Yes, **there were**. / No, **there weren't**.

1 Look at the picture of Fairfield 100 years ago. Complete the sentences with the correct form of *there was/were* and *a/an* or *some/any*.

1 _____ supermarket, but _____ shops.
2 _____ cars in the village, but _____ bikes.
3 _____ cinema, but _____ nightclub.
4 _____ old tree and _____ flowers.

◀ Go back to page 73

9A Present continuous

We use the present continuous to talk about actions that are happening now. We often use time expressions like *at the moment* and *now* with the present continuous.

I'm wearing my new jeans today.
We aren't working at the moment.
What are you doing now?

We form the present continuous with the verb *be* + the *-ing* form of the main verb.

Spelling rules for the *-ing* form
We usually add *-ing* to the infinitive of the verb. *cook* ⇒ *cooking* *watch* ⇒ *watching*
When the verb ends in a consonant + *e*, we usually remove the *e* and then add *-ing*. *take* ⇒ *taking* *dance* ⇒ *dancing*
When the verb ends in a consonant + a vowel + a consonant, we double the consonant and then add *-ing*. *begin* ⇒ *beginning* *get* ⇒ *getting*

▶ 9.3	I	he / she / it	you / we / they
+	I**'m listening** to music.	He**'s reading** a book.	You**'re singing**.
–	I**'m not watching** TV.	She **isn't working**.	We **aren't stopping** here.
?	**Am** I **sleeping**?	**Is** he **studying**?	**Are** they **going**?
Y/N	Yes, I **am**. / No, I**'m not**.	Yes, he **is**. / No, he **isn't**.	Yes, they **are**. / No, they **aren't**.

9C *How often* + expressions of frequency

We use *How often ... ?* + the present simple or the verb *be* to ask about frequency.

How often do you go shopping?
How often does Tim go to London?
How often are you late for class?

We can answer the question *How often ...?* with expressions of frequency.

How often are your English classes?
I have a class once or twice a week. (*once* = one time, *twice* = two times)

▶ 9.13	Expressions of frequency
every day/week/month/year	I go to the gym **every day**.
once a day/week/month/year	John has a holiday **once a year**.
twice a day/week/month/year	Ali has a coffee with his friends **twice a week**.
three/four times a day/week/month/year	They play football **three or four times a month**.

> **Look!** We can also answer questions with *How often ...?* with adverbs of frequency (*always, usually, often, sometimes, never*).
> *How often do you walk to work?*
> *I never walk to work. I usually get the bus.*

1 Write the *-ing* form of the verbs.

1	buy	_____	6	look	_____
2	drive	_____	7	make	_____
3	sit	_____	8	stop	_____
4	go	_____	9	swim	_____
5	leave	_____	10	watch	_____

2 Write positive (+) sentences, negative (–) sentences or questions (?) in the present continuous.

1 George / listen to / music / now (+)

_____

2 you / wear / a new coat (?)

_____

3 she / listen to / me (–)

_____

4 they / do / their homework (–)

_____

5 we / have dinner / at the moment (+)

_____

6 it / rain / today (?)

_____

◀ Go back to page 79

1 Complete the questions and answers. Use the words in brackets.

1 How often _____ your bike? (you / ride)
  I _____ my bike _____ day.
2 How often _____ in your city? (it / snow)
  It only _____ once _____ year.
3 How often _____ his grandparents? (Luis / see)
  He _____ his grandparents three _____ a month.
4 How often _____ tennis? (you / play)
  We _____ tennis _____ weekend.
5 How often _____ their friends? (they / meet)
  They _____ their friends twice _____ week.

◀ Go back to page 83

10A Present continuous for future plans

We use the present continuous to talk about plans and arrangements in the future (for spelling rules of -ing forms see page 104).

I'm going to the dentist next week.

▶ 10.3	I	he / she / it	you / we / they
+	I'**m meeting** friends tonight.	She'**s taking** the bus tomorrow.	You'**re working** next Tuesday.
–	I'**m not going** to school tomorrow.	He **isn't watching** a film tonight.	We **aren't playing** tennis later.
?	**Am** I **working** this weekend?	**Is** she **staying** at home tonight?	**Are** they **going** to the gym?
Y/N	Yes, I **am**. / No, I'**m not**.	Yes, he **is**. / No, he **isn't**.	Yes, they **are**. / No, they **aren't**.

We often use a future time expression to talk about future plans and arrangements. Time expressions usually go at the end of the sentence.

▶ 10.4	Future time expressions
this morning/afternoon/evening	We're taking the train **this afternoon**.
tonight	What are you having for dinner **tonight**?
tomorrow	Sven isn't coming to the party **tomorrow**.
next week/month/year	We're going on holiday **next week**.
later	Are you meeting Jorge **later**?

10C Question review

Questions can be *yes/no* questions or they can ask for specific information with a question word (*where*, *when*, *who*, etc.).

Do you live in Japan?   Yes, I do./No, I don't.
Where are you from?   I'm from Turkey.

For most verbs, the word order in questions is: (question word +) auxiliary verb + subject + main verb + rest of question.

▶ 10.12	(Question word)	Auxiliary verb	Subject	Main verb	Rest of question
Present simple		Does	Chris	speak	English?
	What	do	you	have	for breakfast?
Past simple		Did	Lucy	call	you yesterday?
	When	did	you	arrive	at the airport?
Present continuous		Is	it	snowing	now?
	Where	are	they	going	next week?

For the verbs *be* and *can*, the word order in questions is: (question word +) verb + subject + rest of question.

▶ 10.13	(Question word)	Verb	Subject	Rest of question
be (present simple)		Is	Julia	here?
	Where	are	you	from?
be (past simple)		Were	you	late for work?
	Who	was	Philip	with?
can		Can	you	ride a motorbike?
	What sports	can	they	do?

---

1 Complete the sentences and questions with the present continuous form of the verbs in the box.

> take   not visit   meet
> not come   stay   watch

1 We _____ our friends for dinner later.
2 _____ you _____ the football match tonight?
3 They _____ the 7.30 train to Edinburgh tomorrow.
4 He _____ with some friends in Lima at the weekend.
5 Maria is ill. She _____ to the concert this evening.
6 We _____ the museum next week. It's closed.

2 Write sentences and questions in the present continuous.

1 I / meet / my friends this weekend

_____ .

2 My brother / not visit / us this month

_____ .

3 They / not go / on holiday this summer

_____ .

4 What / you / cook / for dinner on Saturday

_____ ?

◀ Go back to page 87

---

1 Order the words to make questions.

1 rock climbing / does / go / how often / he

_____ ?

2 you / what / for / lunch / are / having

_____ ?

3 homework / when / she / did / do / her

_____ ?

4 can / instrument / you / play / an

_____ ?

5 you / crying / why / are

_____ ?

6 did / where / he / on / go / holiday

_____ ?

7 they / were / home / night / last / at

_____ ?

8 what / is / she / time / leaving

_____ ?

◀ Go back to page 91

6A Places in a town

1 ▶ 6.1 Listen and repeat.

1 bank

2 bus stop

3 café

4 cinema

5 hospital

6 hotel

7 museum

8 nightclub

9 park

10 police station

11 post office

12 restaurant

13 school

14 shopping centre

15 supermarket

16 train station

Look!

a village

a town

a city

A village is small.
A town is medium-sized.
A city is big.

2 Match the places in the box with jobs 1–5.

| hospital police station school |
| restaurant shopping centre |

1 waiter _____
2 police officer _____
3 shop assistant _____
4 teacher _____
5 doctor _____

3 Complete the sentences with the places in the box.

| bank nightclub train station park post office |
| supermarket bus stop café cinema museum |

1 You can send a letter at a _____ .
2 You can get a train at a _____ .
3 You wait for a bus at a _____ .
4 You drink tea or coffee at a _____ .
5 You can dance at a _____ .
6 You watch a film at a _____ .
7 You see interesting things at a _____ .
8 You get money at a _____ .
9 You walk, play games or relax in a _____ .
10 You can buy food and drink at a _____ .

6B Parts of the body

1 ▶ 6.7 Listen and repeat.

1 hair
2 head
3 ear
4 face
5 eye
6 nose
7 tooth (teeth)
8 mouth
9 body
10 arm
11 hand
12 leg
13 knee
14 foot (feet)

Look! The plural of *tooth* is *teeth*.
The plural of *foot* is *feet*.

2 Put the parts of the body in the box in the correct columns.

| arms   body   ears   face   feet   hands   head   knees   legs   mouth   nose   teeth |

I have one ...	I have two ...	I have more than two ...

◀ Go back to page 52

121

6C Rooms and furniture

1 ▶ **6.8** Listen and repeat.

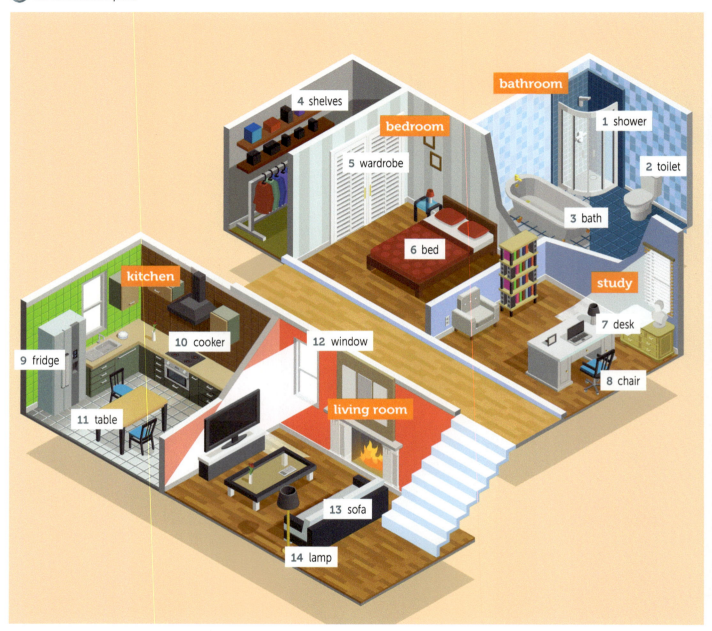

2 Complete the sentences with the rooms and furniture in the box.

> fridge   bath   table   sofa   desk   window   bedroom   cooker   wardrobe   shelves

1 Let's have dinner in the living room. We can sit on the _____ and watch a film.
2 Shona has a big white _____ for all her clothes.
3 My favourite room is the _____ . I sleep there and it's very quiet.
4 After they make dinner, the _____ is very hot.
5 My bathroom is small, so I have a shower, but I don't have a _____ .
6 Ken needs a lot of _____ because he has hundreds of books!
7 It's hot in here. Can you open the _____ ?
8 Please put the milk and orange juice in the _____ .
9 I have a _____ in my bedroom where I do homework and use my laptop.
10 Dinner is ready. The food is on the _____ !

◀ Go back to page 54

7A Celebrities

1 ▶ **7.1** Listen and repeat.

1 artist

2 athlete

3 dancer

4 DJ

5 fashion model

6 film director

7 footballer

8 journalist

9 king

10 musician

11 photographer

12 politician

13 queen

14 racing driver

15 tennis player

16 writer

2 Look at the pictures and complete the sentences with the words in the box.

> fashion model   writer   queen   musician   tennis player   dancer   king   film director   artist   footballer   politician   athlete

1 Shelly-Ann Fraser-Pryce is a Jamaican _____ .

2 Gisele Bündchen is a Brazilian _____

3 Emmanuel Macron is a French _____ .

4 Isabel Allende is a Chilean _____ .

5 Thomas Müller is a German _____ .

6 Margrethe II is the _____ of Denmark.

7 Salvador Dalí was a Spanish _____ .

8 Beyoncé is an American _____ .

9 Sofia Coppola is an American _____ .

10 Venus Williams is an American _____ .

11 Felipe VI is the _____ of Spain.

12 Rudolf Nureyev was a Russian _____ .

◀ Go back to page 60

7B Months and ordinals

1 ▶ 7.5 Listen and repeat.

1 January	2 February	3 March	4 April
5 May	6 June	7 July	8 August
9 September	10 October	11 November	12 December

2 ▶ 7.6 Listen and repeat.

1st	first	7th	seventh	13th	thirteenth	19th	nineteenth
2nd	second	8th	eighth	14th	fourteenth	20th	twentieth
3rd	third	9th	ninth	15th	fifteenth	21st	twenty-first
4th	fourth	10th	tenth	16th	sixteenth	22nd	twenty-second
5th	fifth	11th	eleventh	17th	seventeenth	30th	thirtieth
6th	sixth	12th	twelfth	18th	eighteenth	31st	thirty-first

Look! In British English the ordinal comes before the month.
2 February = the second of February
16 June = the sixteenth of June
But in American English, the ordinal comes after the month.
February 2 = February second
June 16 = June sixteenth

3 Look at the dates in brackets and complete the sentences with the words.

1 St Valentine's Day is the _____ of _____ . (14/02)
2 Independence Day in the USA is the _____ of _____ . (04/07)
3 New Year's Day is the _____ of _____ . (01/01)
4 Halloween is the _____ of _____ . (31/10)
5 My birthday is the _____ of _____ . (25/07)
6 Mother's Day in the UK this year is the _____ of _____ . (11/03)

◀ Go back to page 62

7C Time expressions

1 ▶ 7.14 Listen and repeat.

1 last last night, last week, last year
2 ago two days ago, three weeks ago, four years ago
3 yesterday yesterday morning, yesterday afternoon, yesterday evening
4 times at 9.00, at 11.30, at midnight
5 days on Monday, on Tuesday, at the weekend
6 dates on 1 January, on 24 April, on 11 December
7 years in 1985, in 2001, in 2018
8 decades in the 1960s, in the 1990s, in the 2010s

Look! We say *yesterday morning/afternoon/evening*, but *last night*, NOT ~~yesterday~~ night.

2 Complete the sentences with the words in the box.

| on (x2) in ago last (x2) yesterday at |

1 I studied English _____ morning. Then I watched TV.
2 We enjoyed your party _____ night. It was great!
3 Slavska meets her friends _____ 6.30 after work.
4 I lived in Madrid _____ the 1980s. It was an interesting time.
5 My brother travelled to South America _____ year.
6 I started my new job _____ 4 November.
7 My grandfather played football for Arsenal 50 years _____ .
8 I usually finish work early _____ Friday.

◀ Go back to page 65

8A Travel verbs

1 ▶ 8.1 Listen and repeat.

1 **book** a flight

2 **fly**

3 **get in** a taxi

4 **get lost**

5 **get off** a bus

6 **get on** a train

7 **get out of** a taxi

8 **miss** the bus

9 **ride** a bike

10 **sail**

11 **take** the underground

12 **walk**

2 Tick (✔) the verbs we can use with each type of transport.

	a taxi	a bike	a boat	a plane	a bus	a train
ride						
take						
miss						
get in / out of						
get on / off						
sail						

3 Choose the correct words to complete the sentences.

1 Anne needs to *walk / book* a ticket for her trip to Los Angeles.
2 This is our bus stop. Quick, *get off / get out* now!
3 Let's *walk / get out* home. It's a nice warm evening.
4 Juan decided to *sail / fly* to Spain because he hates planes.
5 When the train arrived, a lot of people tried to *get lost / get on*.

6 There aren't any trains. We need to *ride / take* a taxi home.
7 They *missed / booked* their bus, so they arrived really late.
8 I can drive you home if you want. *Get in / Get out*!
9 Stuart *drives / rides* a motorbike because it's fast.
10 You can *take / ride* the number 35 bus to the city centre.

◀ Go back to page 68

8B Weather and seasons

1 ▶ 8.6 Listen and repeat.

°C
— 40 1 hot
— 30
— 20 2 warm
— 10
— 0   3 cold

4 cloudy   5 sunny   6 wet   7 dry

8 windy   9 foggy   10 rain   11 snow

12 spring   13 summer   14 autumn   15 winter

Look! *rain* and *snow* are verbs. To talk about the weather now, we say *It's raining/ It's snowing*. To talk about the weather in general, we say *It rains/It snows*.

2 Look at the weather map and complete the sentences.

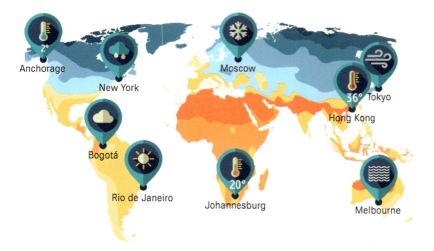

Anchorage
2°
New York
Moscow
Tokyo
36°
Hong Kong
Bogotá
Rio de Janeiro
Johannesburg
20°
Melbourne

1 It's _____ in Moscow.
2 It's _____ in Bogotá.
3 It's _____ in Rio de Janeiro.
4 It's _____ in New York.
5 It's _____ in Tokyo.
6 It's _____ in Hong Kong.
7 It's _____ in Anchorage.
8 It's _____ in Johannesburg.
9 It's _____ in Melbourne.

     ◀ Go back to page 70

8C Nature

1 ▶ 8.7 Listen and repeat.

1 beach

2 cloud

3 field

4 flower

5 forest

6 grass

7 mountain

8 river

9 sea

10 sky

11 sun

12 tree

2 Choose the correct words to complete the sentences.

1 Kilimanjaro is a *beach / mountain* in Tanzania.
2 The Nile is a *river / field* in Africa.
3 The Amazon is a type of *forest / mountain* in South America.
4 The rose is a *cloud / flower* that can be different colours.
5 Jamaica is in the Caribbean *Sea / River*.
6 Copacabana is a *beach / forest* in Brazil.
7 Apples are a fruit that come from a *grass / tree*.
8 The temperature of the *sun / sky* is 15 million °C.
9 Cumulus, Cirrus and Stratus are *clouds / trees*.
10 Animals like horses and rabbits eat *trees / grass*.

◀ Go back to page 72

127

9A Clothes

1 ▶ 9.1 Listen and repeat.

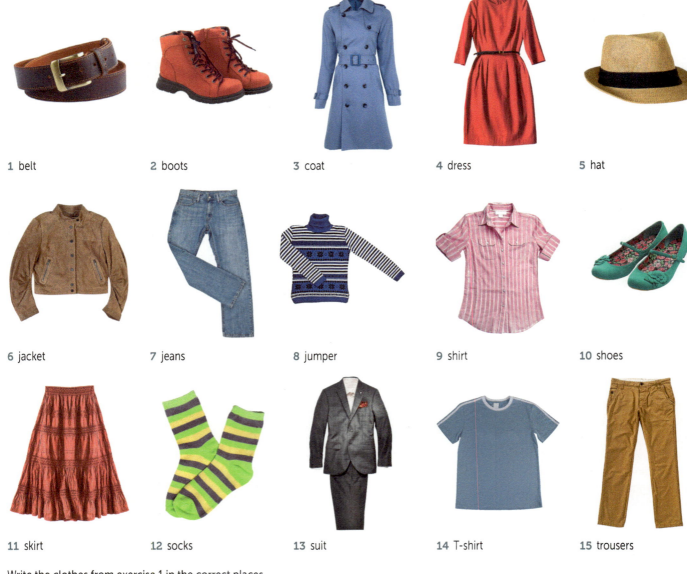

| 1 belt | 2 boots | 3 coat | 4 dress | 5 hat |

| 6 jacket | 7 jeans | 8 jumper | 9 shirt | 10 shoes |

| 11 skirt | 12 socks | 13 suit | 14 T-shirt | 15 trousers |

2 Write the clothes from exercise 1 in the correct places.

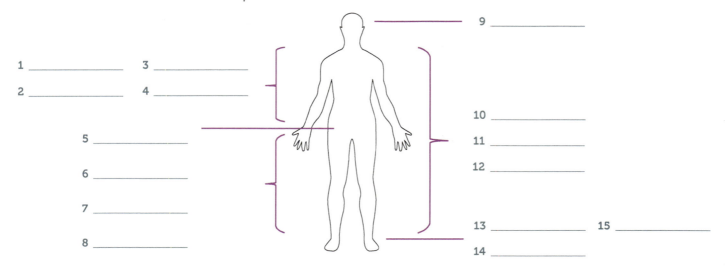

9 _____

1 _____   3 _____

2 _____   4 _____

5 _____

6 _____

7 _____

8 _____

10 _____

11 _____

12 _____

13 _____   15 _____

14 _____

◀ Go back to page 78

9B Feelings

1 ▶ 9.6 Listen and repeat.

1 angry

2 bored

3 calm

4 excited

5 happy

6 hungry

7 sad

8 scared

9 surprised

10 thirsty

11 tired

12 worried

2 Choose the correct adjective to complete the sentences.

1 Can I have a drink of water? I'm really *hungry / thirsty*.
2 He's *surprised / worried* about money because he doesn't have a job.
3 I'm *bored / scared*. This film isn't very interesting.
4 It's Louisa's birthday tomorrow – she's very *excited / tired*.
5 I like yoga because it makes me feel *calm / sad*.
6 Are you *angry / hungry*? Do you want a sandwich?
7 You're very *scared / tired*. Why don't you go to bed?
8 Tim is *angry / hungry* with me because I broke his computer.
9 I was *bored / surprised* that John ran a marathon because he doesn't like sport.
10 Suzie doesn't like horror films. They make her feel *scared / surprised*.

3 Match the feelings in the box with the messages.

| tired sad worried angry surprised |

1 **Julia** I get my exam results today! 😟
2 **Ying-Li** I arrived in London today after a 10-hour flight. 😴
3 **Saanvi** I won the Science competition. I can't believe it! 😱
4 **Dave** All my friends are in Cuba on holiday. I'm at work. 😫
5 **Hans** I lost my wallet on the train today … and I was late for work. 😠

◀ Go back to page 80

9C Shopping

1 ▶ 9.12 Listen and repeat.

1 buy a car

2 go shopping

3 pay by credit card

4 pay with cash

5 sell ice cream

6 shop online

7 spend money

8 try on clothes

9 department store

10 local shops

11 market

12 shopping centre

2 Match the halves to make sentences.

1 I always pay by _____
2 We usually spend _____
3 Can I try on _____
4 I never shop _____
5 Jorge sells _____
6 Malika wants to buy _____
7 You can only pay with _____
8 We need to go _____

a these jeans, please?
b a new laptop.
c fish in the market.
d shopping for food.
e £100 every weekend.
f credit card. It's easy!
g cash in this shop.
h online. I like real shops.

3 Choose the correct words to complete the sentences.

1 I don't *go / buy* shopping on Saturdays. There are lots of people.
2 My brother works for a technology company. He *spends / sells* computers.
3 Sharon lives in a small village. There are only three or four *department stores / local shops*.
4 Carla *spends / buys* all her money on clothes.
5 When we go on holiday, we usually pay *with / by* credit card.
6 The *shopping centre / market* near us has a cinema and lots of restaurants.
7 I always *try / shop* on clothes before I buy them.
8 My mobile phone is broken. I need to *buy / pay* a new one.

◀ Go back to page 82

10A Free-time activities

1 ▶ **10.1** Listen and repeat.

1 go to a concert

2 go to a festival

3 go to the beach

4 have a barbecue

5 have a good time

6 have a party

7 stay at home

8 stay in a hotel

9 stay in a tent

10 visit a museum

11 visit an art gallery

12 visit family/friends

13 watch a film

14 watch a football match

15 watch a video

2 Match the activities in the box with the people.

> visit family   go to the beach   have a barbecue   watch a film
> have a party   stay at home   visit a museum   stay in a tent

1 Erica likes hot weather and swimming. She has two new books to read. _____
2 It's a nice sunny day. Paul is hungry and he has some meat and fish. _____
3 It's Lucia's birthday tomorrow and she wants to celebrate with her friends. _____
4 The weather isn't good and Samuel has an exam next week. _____
5 Marek and Kasia are in London for the weekend. They're interested in history. _____
6 Sonia loves nature. She wants to go on holiday, but she doesn't want to spend a lot of money. _____
7 Cristian is going to San Francisco. His parents and brothers and sisters live there. _____
8 Natalia is at home tonight. She bought a new 102 cm TV last week. _____

◀ Go back to page 86

10B Types of music and film

1 ▶ 10.9 Listen and repeat.

1 classical music

2 electronic music

3 hip-hop music

4 jazz music

5 pop music

6 rock music

7 an action film

8 a comedy

9 a drama

10 a horror film

11 a romance

12 a science-fiction film

2 Look at the pictures and write the types of music and films.

1 _____

2 _____

3 _____

4 _____

5 _____

6 _____

◀ Go back to page 88

10C Sports and games

1 ▶ 10.10 Listen and repeat.

1 do gymnastics

2 do karate

3 do Pilates

4 do yoga

5 go cycling

6 go rock climbing

7 go running

8 go skiing

9 go swimming

10 go walking

11 play basketball

12 play chess

13 play football

14 play hockey

15 play rugby

16 play tennis

17 play videogames

18 play volleyball

> **Look!**
>
> We use *play* with sports that use a ball and with games.
> *I play golf.*
>
> We use *go* with activities that end in *-ing*.
> *I go sailing.*
>
> We use *do* with individual activities and sports that don't use a ball.
> *I do judo.*

2 Complete the sentences with the correct form of *go*, *play* or *do*.

1 He usually _____ tennis at the weekend.
2 It's a lovely sunny day. Why don't we _____ walking?
3 They _____ gymnastics every Monday after school.
4 Do you want to _____ chess later?

5 Did you _____ cycling last weekend?
6 She often _____ Pilates to relax.
7 I _____ skiing with my parents every winter.
8 Do your children _____ a lot of videogames?

◀ Go back to page 90

6A Student A

Look at the picture. Ask and answer questions with Student B to find six differences.

A *Are there any hotels?*
B *Yes, there are. There are two hotels.*
A *In my picture, there's one hotel.*
B *Is there a cinema?*

6C Student A

1 Describe your picture to Student B. He/She will draw it.

A *There's a bed. Next to the bed, there's a small table.*

2 Listen to Student B and draw the room.

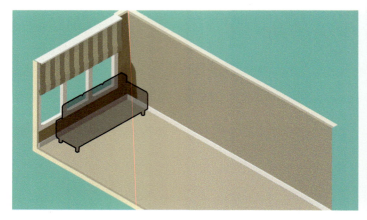

6D Student A

1 Ask Student B for directions to the places in the box. Listen and mark on the map where they are. Check the information if you need to.

> post office   bank   Internet café

> A *Excuse me, is there a post office near here?*
> B *Yes, there is. You go down Market Street ...*
> A *Could you repeat that, please?*

2 Listen to Student B. Look at the map and give directions.

7A Student A

1 Ask Student B questions with *was* to match the celebrities with their jobs and where they were from.

> A *Was Federico Fellini an artist?*
> B *No, he wasn't.*

1	Federico Fellini	writer	South Africa
2	Janis Joplin	politician	the USA
3	Nelson Mandela	film director	Colombia
4	Greta Garbo	artist	Japan
5	Katsushika Hokusai	singer	Italy
6	Gabriel García Márquez	actor	Sweden

2 Answer Student B's questions about the celebrities. You can only say *Yes, he/she was* or *No, he/she wasn't*.

1 Frida Kahlo was an artist from Mexico.
2 Johan Cruyff was a footballer from the Netherlands.
3 Celia Cruz was a singer from Cuba.
4 Jane Austen was a writer from the UK.
5 Paco de Lucía was a musician from Spain.
6 Jawaharlal Nehru was a politician from India.

7C Student A

1 Ask Student B questions. Find one incorrect piece of information for each person.

> A *Did Luke visit his grandparents last week?*
> B *No, he didn't. He visited his grandparents last month.*

1 Luke / visit / his grandparents / last ~~week~~   month
2 Kenny / travel / to Brazil / three years ago
3 Clara / play / volleyball / yesterday
4 Debbie / cook / noodles / last night
5 Steve / work / as a teacher / in the 1980s
6 Amelia / watch / a TV show / yesterday morning

2 Listen to Student B's questions. Correct the information.

1 Zoe stayed in a hotel in the city centre last year.
2 Jim studied Spanish at university in the 1990s.
3 Antonia walked 30 kilometres yesterday.
4 Leandro watched a football match three days ago.
5 Rachel started a new job in London last month.
6 Tom finished work one hour ago.

7A London's famous houses: answers

1 Mahatma Gandhi

2 Bob Marley

3 Agatha Christie

4 Vincent van Gogh

8A Student A

1 Ask Student B questions to find out what Lola did yesterday.

A *Where did Lola go?*
B *She went to her dad's birthday party.*

Lola	Where / go?
	What time / leave / the house?
	she / take / the bus?
	What / wear?
	What / buy / for her dad?
	she / have / a good time?
	Where / sleep / last night?

2 Read the information and answer Student B's questions about what Mateo did yesterday.

Mateo	He / go / Rome
	He / fly
	He / take / taxi to the airport
	His flight / leave at 11.00 a.m.
	He / go / with friends
	He / sleep / on a plane for 20 minutes
	He / have / a good journey

8C Student A

1 Look at the picture for one minute. Then close your book and answer Student B's questions.

2 Give Student B one minute to look at his/her picture. Ask him/her questions with *Was/Were there a/an/any …?* and the words in the box. If he/she answers *Yes, there were*, ask *How many were there?*

boats	hospital	cars	flowers
birds	shops	beach	river

A *Were there any boats?*   B *Yes, there were.*
A *How many were there?*   B *There was one boat.*

8D Student A

1 Read the situation in the box, then look at the flowchart. You are the receptionist. Student B calls you. Have the conversation.

A *Hello, Green Lane Medical Centre. Jorge speaking. How can I help you?*
B *Hello, my name's Anna Lopez. I'd like to see the doctor.*

> You work at the Green Lane Medical Centre. Answer the phone. Ask the person what the problem is.

Receptionist

Answer the phone. Give the name of the medical centre/sports centre and your name.

Patient/Customer

Introduce yourself and say why you are calling.

Ask more detailed questions.

Answer.

Ask for the caller's contact details.

Answer.

Finish the call.

2 Read the situation in the box, then look at the flowchart again. You are the customer. Call Student B and have the conversation.

> You want to join a sports centre. You're interested in swimming and tennis. Your phone number is 07700 900382.

9C Student A

Ask and answer the question *How often do/does ...?* with Student B to complete the table.

A *How often do Jon and Andy go to the cinema?*
B *They go to the cinema three or four times a year.*

Laura	have dinner in a restaurant	twice a month
Jon and Andy	go to the cinema	
Carlota	shop online	once or twice a week
Ahmed	ride a motorbike	
Hope and Sara	check their emails	four or five times a day
Igor	read a new book	
Luisa and Raul	go swimming	every week
Yannis	go on holiday	

10A Student A

Look at your diary. Try to find a time when you can meet Student B. Ask and answer the question *What are you doing on ...?* for the different days.

A *What are you doing on Monday morning?*
B *I'm going to the gym. What about Monday afternoon?*

	Monday	Tuesday	Wednesday	Thursday	Friday
Morning			travel to the city		
Afternoon	see doctor	have lunch with parents	visit National Museum		
Evening	watch film at cinema		stay with friends		have dinner with Carl

10C Student A

Ask Student B questions about his/her hobby in the correct tense. Write down his/her answers. Then guess what the hobby is.

A *How often do you do your hobby?*
B *I do it twice a week.*

	Student B's hobby	Your hobby: rock climbing
1 How often / you / do / your hobby?		Every weekend.
2 When / you / start?		When I was 14.
3 it / be / expensive?		No, it isn't.
4 it / be / dangerous?		It can be.
5 you / play / it in a team?		No, but I always go with another person.
6 How many people / be there / in your team?		–
7 Where / you / do / your hobby?		Sometimes at a sports centre, sometimes in the mountains.
8 you / do / your hobby next weekend?		Yes, I'm driving to the beach on Friday night.

6A Student B

Look at the picture. Ask and answer questions with Student A to find six differences.

B *Are there any hotels?*
A *Yes, there are. There's one hotel.*
B *In my picture, there are two hotels.*
A *Is there a cinema?*

6C Student B

1 Listen to Student A and draw the room.

A *There's a bed. Next to the bed, there's a small table.*

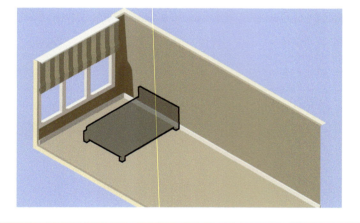

2 Describe your picture to Student A. He/She will draw it.

B *There's a sofa in front of the window.*

6D Student B

1 Listen to Student A. Look at the map and give directions.

A *Excuse me, is there a post office near here?*
B *Yes, there is. You go down Market Street ...*
A *Could you repeat that, please?*

2 Ask Student A for directions to the places in the box. Listen and mark on the map where they are. Check the information if you need to.

> restaurant
> tourist information office
> supermarket

7A Student B

1 Answer Student A's questions about the celebrities. You can only say *Yes, he/she was* or *No, he/she wasn't.*

A *Was Federico Fellini an artist?*
B *No, he wasn't.*
1 Federico Fellini was a film director from Italy.
2 Janis Joplin was a singer from the USA.
3 Nelson Mandela was a politician from South Africa.
4 Greta Garbo was an actor from Sweden.
5 Katsushika Hokusai was an artist from Japan.
6 Gabriel García Márquez was a writer from Colombia.

2 Ask Student A questions with *was* to match the celebrities with their jobs and where they were from.

1	Frida Kahlo	footballer	India
2	Johan Cruyff	musician	Spain
3	Celia Cruz	politician	Mexico
4	Jane Austen	singer	the Netherlands
5	Paco de Lucía	writer	Cuba
6	Jawaharlal Nehru	artist	the UK

7C Student B

1 Listen to Student A's questions. Correct the information.

A *Did Luke visit his grandparents last week?*
B *No, he didn't. He visited his grandparents last month.*
1 Luke visited his grandparents last month.
2 Kenny travelled to Brazil six years ago.
3 Clara played basketball yesterday.
4 Debbie cooked rice last night.
5 Steve worked as a teacher in the 1970s.
6 Amelia watched a film yesterday morning.

2 Ask Student A questions. Find one incorrect piece of information for each person.

1 Zoe / stay / in a hotel near the beach / last year
2 Jim / study / German at university / in the 1990s
3 Antonia / walk / 30 kilometres / two days ago
4 Leandro / watch / a football match / last week
5 Rachel / start / a new job in Paris / last month
6 Tom / finish / work / half an hour ago

9C Questionnaire results

Mostly as: You don't like shopping and you hate shopping centres. You prefer to spend money on other things. What do you do and how often do you do it?

Mostly bs: You like shopping, but you also like doing other things. A shopping centre is a good place to meet friends. How often do you go there?

Mostly cs: You love shopping – it's your life. You go shopping two or three times a week and you shop online almost every day ... but do you really need to buy all those things?

8A Student B

1 Read the information and answer Student A's questions about what Lola did yesterday.

A *Where did Lola go?*   B *She went to her dad's birthday party.*

Lola	
	She / go / her dad's birthday party
	She / leave / the house at 7.00 p.m.
	She / take / the train
	She / wear / a new dress
	She / buy / a book
	She / have / a good time
	She / sleep / on her dad's sofa

2 Ask Student A questions to find out what Mateo did yesterday.

Mateo	
	Where / he / go?
	he / go / by train?
	he / take / a taxi to the airport?
	what time / his flight / leave?
	he / go / with friends?
	he / sleep / on the plane?
	he / have / a good journey?

8C Student B

1 Give Student A one minute to look at his/her picture. Ask him/her questions with *Was/Were there a/an/any ...?* and the words in the box. If he/she answers *Yes, there were*, ask *How many were there?*

people   clouds   forest   trees
bus   houses   cars   river

B *Were there any people?*   A *Yes, there were.*
B *How many were there?*   A *There were four people.*

2 Look at the picture for one minute. Then close your book and answer Student A's questions.

8D Student B

1 Read the situation in the box, then look at the flowchart. You are the patient. Call Student A and have the conversation.

A *Hello, Green Lane Medical Centre. Jorge speaking. How can I help you?*
B *Hello, my name's Anna Lopez. I'd like to see the doctor.*

You don't feel well and want to see the doctor. Your head hurts. Your phone number is 01632 960785.

Receptionist

Answer the phone. Give the name of the medical centre/sports centre and your name.

Patient/Customer

Introduce yourself and say why you are calling.

Ask more detailed questions.

Answer.

Ask for the caller's contact details.

Answer.

Finish the call.

2 Read the situation in the box, then look at the flowchart again. You are the receptionist. Student A calls you. Have the conversation.

You work at a sports centre called The Fitness Factory. Answer the phone. Ask the person what sports they want to do.

9A Student B

Look at the picture. Describe James, Grace and Kara to Student A. Try to find six differences.

B *Grace is wearing a red dress and boots.*
A *In my picture, she's wearing shoes.*

9C Student B

Ask and answer the question *How often do/does …?* with Student A to complete the table.

B *How often does Laura have dinner in a restaurant?*
A *She has dinner in a restaurant twice a month.*

Laura	have dinner in a restaurant	
Jon and Andy	go to the cinema	three or four times a year
Carlota	shop online	
Ahmed	ride a motorbike	every day
Hope and Sara	check their emails	
Igor	read a new book	four or five times a year
Luisa and Raul	go swimming	
Yannis	go on holiday	once a year

10A Student B

Look at your diary. Try to find a time when you can meet Student A. Ask and answer the question *What are you doing on …?* for the different days.

A *What are you doing on Monday morning?*
B *I'm going to the gym. What about Monday afternoon?*

	Monday	Tuesday	Wednesday	Thursday	Friday
Morning	go to the gym	meet Simon for coffee		take bus to city	see dentist
Afternoon				visit art gallery	
Evening		go to a concert		stay in hotel	

9A Student A

Look at the picture. Describe Aziz, Oscar and Petra to Student B. Try to find six differences.

A *Aziz is looking at a white hat.*
B *In my picture, he's looking at some sunglasses.*

Petra   Aziz   Oscar   Grace   James   Kara

10C Student B

Ask Student A questions about his/her hobby in the correct tense. Write down his/her answers. Then guess what the hobby is.

B *How often do you do your hobby?*
A *I do it every weekend.*

	Student A's hobby	Your hobby: basketball
1 How often / you / do / your hobby?		Twice a week.
2 When / you / start?		Last year.
3 it / be / expensive?		No, it isn't.
4 it / be / dangerous?		No, it isn't.
5 you / play / it in a team?		Yes, I do.
6 How many people / be there / in your team?		12 (but only five play at the same time).
7 Where / you / do / your hobby?		At the sports centre.
8 you / do / your hobby next weekend?		Yes, we're going to Los Angeles for a match.

10D Students A and B

1 Complete the sentences. You can use real information or invent it.

About me
In my free time, I often _____ .
My favourite type of music is _____ .
Last weekend
I went shopping on Saturday and I bought _____
_____ .
Last weekend, I _____ .

My holidays
Last summer, I went to _____ .
When I'm on holiday, I usually _____ .
My plans
Next weekend, I'm meeting _____ .
For my next holiday, I'm _____ .

2 Read your sentences in pairs. Respond with interest using the words in the box.

> Oh really?   That's interesting.   That sounds good.   Wow, that's amazing!   Cool!   Great!

A *In my free time, I often go skiing in the mountains.*
B *Wow, that's amazing!*

Irregular verbs

Infinitive	Past simple
be	was, were
become	became
begin	began
break	broke
bring	brought
buy	bought
choose	chose
come	came
cost	cost
do	did
drink	drank
drive	drove
eat	ate
fall	fell
feel	felt
find	found
fly	flew
get	got
give	gave
go	went
have	had
hear	heard
hold	held
hurt	hurt
keep	kept
know	knew
learn	learnt/learned

Infinitive	Past simple
leave	left
lose	lost
make	made
meet	met
pay	paid
put	put
read (/riːd/)	read (/red/)
ride	rode
run	ran
say	said
see	saw
sell	sold
sit	sat
sleep	slept
spend	spent
speak	spoke
stand	stood
swim	swam
take	took
teach	taught
tell	told
think	thought
understand	understood
wake	woke
wear	wore
win	won
write	wrote

Personal Best

Workbook

A1
Beginner

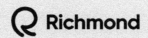

GRAMMAR: *there is / are*

1 ▶6.1 Complete the conversation with the words in the box. Listen and check.

there are some	there's an	are there any
is there a	there aren't any	is there an
there isn't a	there aren't	

A In this picture, ¹ _there are some_ pencils.
B ² _____ pen.
A ³ _____ book? Yes, look!
B ⁴ _____ glasses, too. Reading glasses.
A ⁵ _____ sunglasses.
B But ⁶ _____ umbrella.
A ⁷ _____ wallet.
B ⁸ _____ credit cards?
A Credit cards? No, ⁹ _____.
B ¹⁰ _____ key? Yes, one.
A ¹¹ _____ camera.
B But ¹² _____ mobile phones – two!

2 Read the information about Nuuk, the capital of Greenland. Then complete the text with *there is/there are*, and *a/an*, *some* or *any*.

population	17,000	shopping centres	1
airports	1	cafés & restaurants	10+
schools	5+	art galleries	?
big hotels	1	discos	?
roads out of town	0	boats and ferries	100s!
parks	0		

Nuuk is the capital of Greenland, but it only has 17,000 people. ¹ _There's an_ airport and ² _____ schools. ³ _____ big hotel but ⁴ _____ roads out of Nuuk and ⁵ _____ parks. ⁶ _____ shopping centre and ⁷ _____ cafés and restaurants. ⁸ _____ art gallery? I don't think so. What about discos? ⁹ _____ discos? I'm not sure. But I know that ¹⁰ _____ boats and ferries – lots of them!

VOCABULARY: Places in a town

3 Order the letters to make places in a town.

1 s t o p f e c i o f _____
2 h a i l s p o t _____
3 i c e m a n _____
4 t h i n g b u l c _____
5 l e p i c o n a t t o s i _____
6 s k a t e r u m p e r _____
7 r a n t i o s t i n a t _____
8 u s e m u m _____

4 Complete the sentences with places in a town.

1 buy clothes, computers, sunglasses, books, etc. in a _____ _____
2 catch the bus at the _____ _____
3 eat in a _____ or _____
4 keep your money in a _____
5 sleep in a _____
6 catch a plane from the _____
7 walk your dog in the _____
8 learn English at a language _____

PRONUNCIATION: Linking consonants and vowels

5 ▶6.2 Listen and repeat the sentences. Pay attention to how the sounds link together.

1 There‿are some cafés.
2 There's‿a restaurant.
3 Is there‿a shopping centre?
4 Yes, there‿is. There‿are some shops, too.
5 There‿isn't‿a school.
6 There‿aren't‿any offices.
7 Are there‿any parks?
8 No, there‿aren't.

READING: Reading in detail

1 Read the article. Who thinks the city is a good place to live – Ursula or Lenny? Who thinks the countryside is a good place to live? Whose opinion do you agree with, Ursula's or Lenny's?

BIG CITY or COUNTRYSIDE?

Where is a better place to live? We ask two friends to give their opinions.

Ursula Is life exciting in the city? In my view, travelling an hour to work every day is not exciting. Also, it isn't expensive in the countryside. Small apartments in big cities are expensive.

People say that it's boring here because it's difficult to find things to do. But I like going for walks and learning about animals and birds. There's lots to do in the city, but I don't think theatres and museums are interesting.

Finally, people are friendly in the countryside. We say 'hi' to everyone. Not like in cities!

Lenny The countryside is a great place to live ... if you are old! Why live in a place where you need a car because the cinema is 20 km away?

Also, there aren't many good jobs and the only social life is online. In my opinion, cities are interesting for young people because everything you need is right there.

Also, you don't need a car because you can walk or cycle. So city life is good for you and the planet.

2 Read the article again. Choose Yes (Y) or No (N). Write the word or phrase in the article that gives you the answer. Use the <u>underlined</u> key words to help you.

1 Does Ursula <u>know</u> Lenny? (Y) / N _friends_
2 Does Ursula think life is <u>exciting in the city</u>? Y / N _____
3 Are there <u>many things to do in the city</u>, in Ursula's opinion? Y / N _____
4 In Ursula's opinion, are <u>cities unfriendly</u>? Y / N _____
5 Does Lenny say cars <u>are necessary in the countryside</u>? Y / N _____
6 Does Lenny think the <u>countryside is good for young people</u>? Y / N _____
7 Does Lenny like to have <u>cinemas, supermarkets, etc. near him</u>? Y / N _____

3 Match the two parts of the sentences.

1 Ursula doesn't like _____   a cities are boring.
2 She doesn't think that the _____   b good places to live.
3 She likes _____   c going for walks.
4 Lenny doesn't think _____   d interesting things to do in cities.
5 He thinks there are _____   e long journeys to work.
6 In his view, cities are _____   f countryside is boring.

4 Complete the parts of the body.

1 It's easy to see where something is with two e__ __ __ on the front of our f__ __ __.
2 Our e__ __ __ are on the side of our h__ __ __.
3 There are 32 t__ __ __ __ in an adult's m__ __ __ __, but only 20 in a child's.
4 Your h__ __ __ __ and f__ __ __ are at the end of your arms and legs.
5 Our h__ __ __ helps to keep us warm!
6 We use our n__ __ __ to smell things like food.
7 You can look after your b__ __ __ by eating healthy food and doing exercise.
8 Running long distances can be bad for your k__ __ __.

GRAMMAR: Prepositions of place

1 Choose the correct prepositions to complete the sentences.

1 My pen is _____ your chair. Can you give it to me?
   a between   **b** in   **c** under

2 The children's bedroom is very small so they have 'bunk beds' – one bed is _____ the other.
   a above   **b** next to   **c** behind

3 I think that new lamp looks good _____ the computer and the window.
   a on   **b** under   **c** between

4 We have a bed, a chair and a table _____ our bedroom.
   a in   **b** above   **c** next to

5 Why is the television _____ the desk? We can't watch a film like that!
   a in front of **b** between   **c** behind

6 There's a beautiful park _____ our flat. You can see it from our living room.
   a above   **b** in front of **c** in

7 Please put the salad _____ the table for our lunch.
   a on   **b** under   **c** next to

8 The train station is _____ the shops. Go through the shopping centre and you can see it on the other side.
   a under   **b** behind   **c** above

2 Complete the sentences with the correct prepositions.

1 Come and sit _____ to me. We can do our homework together.

2 Please don't stand in _____ of the fridge. I need the milk and some eggs.

3 I can't see my car – it's _____ the house. But I'm sure it's there!

4 He keeps his keys _____ his wallet so he doesn't lose them.

5 It's raining. Do you want to stand _____ my umbrella with me?

6 Is the nightclub _____ the cinema and the bank?

7 Planes fly _____ our town all day. It's very noisy sometimes!

8 Don't put your dirty feet _____ the table!

VOCABULARY: Rooms and furniture

3 Look at the words in the box. Order the letters then write the words in the correct rooms.

~~deb~~	fosa	roceko	herows
bhat	ittelo	beardrow	

bedroom	bathroom
bed	_____
_____	_____
_____	_____
kitchen	**living room**
_____	_____

4 Look at the picture. Complete the description.

This is my ¹_____. I do my homework here. I have my laptop on this ²_____. There's a large ³_____ above it so I have lots of light in the day. But in the evening, I put on my ⁴_____ next to the computer. I have lots of books, so there are some long ⁵_____ between the desk and this ⁶_____. My ⁷_____ is very old, so I sometimes sit on the sofa to study. But my favourite thing? I have a small ⁸_____ under my desk with cold drinks and chocolate. It's my mini-kitchen!

PRONUNCIATION: Sentence stress

5 ▶ 6.3 Underline the stressed words. Listen and check.

1 My desk is under the window.

2 The table is next to the shelves.

3 Their bathroom is above the kitchen.

4 The chair is between the bed and the wardrobe.

5 His keys are on the chair.

6 Our sofa is in the living room.

SPEAKING: Asking for and giving directions

1 ▶ 6.4 Listen to three conversations. Where do the people want to go?

1 The woman wants to go to the _____.
2 The man wants to go to the _____.
3 The man wants to go to the _____.

2 ▶ 6.4 Listen again and complete the conversations.

Conversation 1

1 _____ me, _____ the park, please?

2 Go _____ this street and turn _____ at the hospital.

Conversation 2

3 Is _____ a police station around _____?

4 _____ right before the post office. You can see it _____ the post office, on the _____.

Conversation 3

5 Is the museum _____ here?

6 Go down _____ street for about three or four _____ and then turn right _____ the shopping centre.

3 ▶ 6.5 Listen to the conversation. Which place does the man call?

a the post office
b the cinema
c the swimming pool

4 ▶ 6.6 Listen again to six extracts from the conversation in exercise 3. Match each extract with the ways of checking information (a–c).

1 _____
2 _____
3 _____
4 _____
5 _____
6 _____

a asking someone to repeat
b asking someone to speak more slowly
c asking a question to check the information

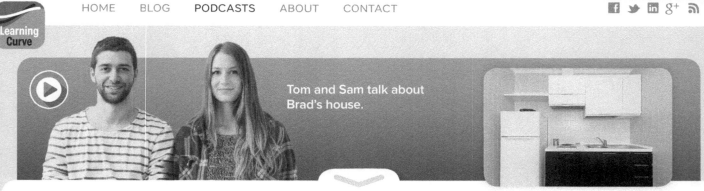

Learning Curve

Tom and Sam talk about Brad's house.

LISTENING

1 ▶ **6.7** Listen to the podcast about a very small house. Tick (✔) the things Brad has in his house.

a cooker   _____
b table   _____
c sofa   _____
d chair   _____
e desk   _____
f bath   _____
g shower   _____
h toilet   _____
i wardrobe   _____
j bed   _____

2 ▶ **6.7** Listen again. Write T (true), F (false), or NG (not given) if there is no information in the podcast.

1 Tom says that Sam has lots of parties.   _____
2 There are thirteen small houses near Brad.   _____
3 Brad has a large garden at the front of his house.   _____
4 Brad cooks every day.   _____
5 There are four chairs in the living room.   _____
6 Brad's friends visit him on Saturdays.   _____
7 Brad prefers showers to baths.   _____
8 Brad's bed is in the wardrobe.   _____
9 Brad pays £600 each month for his house.   _____
10 Brad wants to live in a different house when he is older.   _____

READING

1 Read Penny's blog about New York. Choose the correct sentence.

a The three places are all free.
b You can see art at all these places.
c All the places are very old.

2 Read the blog again. Match the sentences with places a–c.

1 People from other countries don't often go here.   _____
2 You don't need money to visit this place.   _____
3 There are good places to eat here.   _____
4 You can see films here.   _____
5 It isn't near the centre of New York.   _____
6 You can see water from here.   _____

   a the High Line   b the Cloisters
   c Williamsburg

3 Complete the sentences with places in a town.

1 Is there a p _ _ _ o _ _ _ _ e near here? I need to buy some stamps.
2 Daisy broke her leg and had to go to the h _ _ _ _ _ _ l.
3 Let's go to a n _ _ _ _ _ _ b this evening and go dancing!
4 Can you go to the s _ _ _ _ _ _ _ _ _ t and buy some bread and milk, please?
5 Shall we get our tickets online or from the t _ _ _ _ s _ _ _ _ _ n?
6 We stayed in a really expensive h_ _ _ l when we visited Barcelona.
7 I usually buy my Christmas presents in the s _ _ _ _ _ _ g c _ _ _ _ e in town.
8 Nick left his wallet on the bus and had to go to the p _ _ _ _ e s _ _ _ _ _ n.
9 Which s _ _ _ _ l do his children go to?
10 I spent all my money so I went to the b _ _ k to get some more.

HOME   **BLOG**   PODCASTS   ABOUT   CONTACT

This week's guest blogger Penny writes about the New York presenters' favourite places.

Enjoying the 'Big Apple'

At the New York studio we're really lucky to live in a fantastic city with lots to see and do. There are several parks and museums and there are so many restaurants and cafés. It's not easy to choose, but I want to tell you about our favourite places in the city.

Penny

My favourite place is the High Line, a new park in Midtown Manhattan. Before, it was a train line, but now it is a park above the city, about two kilometres long. I love walking, and this is a great place to walk. And there are amazing views of the city and the Hudson River. There are also many plants and flowers to look at on the way, and some very good street art, all free. There are lots of different entrances but the easiest for me is between 12th and 11th Avenues. I often go at the weekend, when I have time.

I love a museum called the Cloisters, in north Manhattan. Not many tourists know about it and it is quite far from the city centre. But it's easy to travel there because there is a bus stop next to it. It's about $25 to get in so I don't go very often. But it's fantastic! At the centre is a really old building and there's lots of beautiful old art to see. And there are some very nice gardens in front of the castle. I like going there because it's very quiet.

Ethan

Marc

At the weekend I sometimes go to Williamsburg in Brooklyn. It's an exciting part of the city, where you can go to fantastic cafés or just walk around the markets and enjoy the atmosphere. I love looking at the street art. There is also a great cinema on Grand Street. There are seven screens and seats for nearly 1,000 people! People from all over the world live in Williamsburgh, and everyone is really friendly. If you want to go shopping, it's great for fresh food and old clothes.

These are our favourite places, but what about you? Tell us about your favourite places in your city!

All in the past

GRAMMAR: Past simple: *be*

1 Complete the sentences with *was, were, wasn't* or *weren't*.

1 Where _____ you on Tuesday?

2 Oh good. You have your mobile phone. Where _____ it?

3 The film _____ very good. Don't go and see it.

4 My grandmother _____ a doctor when most doctors _____ men.

5 The children _____ very noisy yesterday. I hope they're quiet today.

6 The windows are open now, but they _____ this morning.

7 We _____ in bed until after 2 a.m. I'm really tired today!

8 My hair _____ brown when I _____ a baby. It's black now.

9 '_____ Lucy at the party?' 'Yes, she _____.'

10 '_____ you bored in hospital?' 'No, I _____. I read some good books.'

2 Rewrite the sentences and questions in the past simple.

1 I am a taxi driver.
   I was a taxi driver. _____

2 He isn't with us. He's at the shopping centre.
   _____

3 Those students are not very friendly. They are unfriendly.
   _____

4 She isn't at home. She's at the park.
   _____

5 'Are the pizzas cheap?' 'Yes, they are.'
   _____

6 'I'm not very happy.' 'I am!'
   _____

7 'Are your exams difficult?' 'No, they aren't.'
   _____

8 'Is she your teacher?' 'No, she isn't.'
   _____

9 Sam isn't in class this week. He's on holiday.
   _____

10 'Is this question difficult to understand?' 'No, it isn't.'
   _____

VOCABULARY: Celebrities

3 Match the celebrity words with a or b.

1 artist _____
2 athlete _____
3 DJ _____
4 film director _____   **a** arts and entertainment
5 footballer _____
6 musician _____   **b** sports
7 racing driver _____
8 writer _____

4 Complete the words for celebrities.

1 Most f __ __ __ __ __ __ m __ __ __ __ __ are young and beautiful.

2 P__ __ __ __ __ __ __ __ __ __ are public people but they aren't celebrities. They help people but aren't always famous.

3 He works for *The Daily Planet* newspaper and is an excellent j__ __ __ __ __ __ __ __ __.

4 Were the k__ __ __ and q __ __ __ __ of Spain in London last week?

5 I love my work as a ballet d__ __ __ __ __ but the shows are difficult!

6 Now we can all be good p__ __ __ __ __ __ __ __ __ __ __ __ with a digital camera.

7 She wants to be a famous t__ __ __ __ __ p __ __ __ __ __ and win Wimbledon one day!

8 Do you find paintings by the Mexican a__ __ __ __ __ Diego Rivera interesting?

PRONUNCIATION: *was/were*

5 ▶ **7.1** Listen and repeat the questions and answers. Pay attention to the pronunciation of *was* and *were*.

1 **A** Where was he yesterday?
   B He was at home.
2 **A** Where were you on Friday?
   B I was at the post office.
3 **A** Where were they last week?
   B They were in Italy.
4 **A** Where was your sister in June?
   B She was with my grandparents.
5 **A** Where was I on Saturday night?
   B You were at the nightclub.
6 **A** Where were your parents in 1980?
   B They were at university.

LISTENING: Listening for dates

1 ▶ 7.2 Listen to the information. Match the celebrities with three of the words in the box.

actor	dancer	king	musician	politician
queen	sports player		travel writer	

1 Ira Aldridge _____

2 Kumar Shri Ranjitsinhji _____

3 Isabella Bird _____

2 ▶ 7.2 Listen again. Complete the information about each person.

1 These three celebrities were famous in the _____ century.

2 Aldridge was in Britain from _____ until _____.

3 He was alive from 24th July, 1807 until _____ _____ _____.

4 Ranjitsinhji was on an English university team in the year _____.

5 His first national game for England was on _____ _____ _____.

6 Bird was _____ years old when she started travelling.

7 Her first book was in _____.

8 She was _____ years old when she was in Morocco.

3 ▶ 7.3 Listen and complete the sentences.

1 _____ _____ athlete.

2 The _____ is called '_____ _____ _____'.

3 Before she _____ _____ artist, she _____ _____ _____ assistant.

4 My _____ _____ _____ _____ on Fridays and Saturdays.

5 He was born on the twenty-_____ _____ 1987.

6 The last time I _____ _____ a concert was _____ _____ in May.

4 Write the correct dates.

1 4/3 is the fourth of ~~May~~.   *March*

2 15/8 is the fifth of August.   _____

3 10/4 is the second of April.   _____

4 2/1 is the twelfth of January.   _____

5 30/10 is the thirtieth of November.   _____

6 21/7 is the twenty-first of June.   _____

7 6/2 is the fifth of February.   _____

8 9/9 is the nineteenth of September.   _____

GRAMMAR: Past simple: regular verbs

1 Order the words to make questions.

1 live / you / in the 2000s / did / where

_____?

2 did / listen to / music / you / then

_____?

3 was / your / favourite / singer / who

_____?

4 they / did / sing / what

_____?

5 an instrument / did / play / you

_____?

6 the name of / what / your band / was

_____?

2 Complete the sentences and questions. Use the verbs in brackets in the past simple.

1 In South America we _____ (visit) Argentina, Chile and Peru.

2 '_____ (you/travel) to Berlin last year?' 'Yes, I _____.'

3 I _____ (not/watch) the match. Was it good?

4 She _____ (study) all day and all night before her final exam.

5 '_____ (he/arrive) at work on time this morning?' 'No, _____. He was late again!'

6 After school they _____ (listen) to music.

7 We _____ (cook) chicken and vegetables for dinner yesterday.

8 '_____ (she/use) the remote control this morning?' 'Yes, _____.'

9 We _____ (not/like) the furniture in our hotel room.

10 The train journey was very long! The train _____ (stop) at lots of stations.

VOCABULARY: Time expressions

3 Which word does not make a time expression with the underlined word?

1 last month / morning / night / year

2 at six o'clock / the 10th of February / the weekend / 5.30 pm

3 in 1997 / the last decade / last year / the sixties

4 on 2004 / Wednesday / 16 July / Saturday

5 two fifteen / days / weeks / years ago

6 yesterday morning / afternoon / evening / night

7 on / last / in / this Monday

8 three weeks / a year / half an hour / Wednesday ago

4 Complete the sentences with time expressions.

1 We worked until 2.00 a.m. last _____. We're very tired this morning!

2 When did I lose my passport? About 24 hours ago, so _____ afternoon.

3 She got her first job _____ 2012 and she works for the same company today.

4 Where was your summer holiday _____ year?

5 His computer stopped working _____ two o'clock this afternoon.

6 I met my girlfriend three months _____ at the bus stop!

7 They bought the Sat Nav _____ Tuesday and now it doesn't work.

8 Did your mother and father meet in _____ 1980s?

9 My birthday is _____ 24th January.

10 Did they go cycling _____ the weekend?

PRONUNCIATION: -ed endings

5 ▶ 7.4 Complete stories 1–3 with sentences a–i. The -ed endings of the verbs in bold are pronounced the same in each story (/d/, /t/ or /ɪd/). Then listen, check and repeat.

1 Debbie **loved** trains.

___ ___ ___

2 Edwina **needed** to go to the shopping centre.

___ ___ ___

3 Tina **watched** a film in the afternoon.

___ ___ ___

a Then in the evening she **cooked** dinner.

b Last week she **travelled** to Manchester.

c She met a friend there and they **played** tennis.

d She **wanted** to buy a present for her boyfriend.

e She **tried** to win but her friend was very good.

f But she was sad so she **walked** to a disco.

g But everything was expensive and it **started** to rain.

h She **danced** all night there with her friends.

i She **visited** her brother instead.

WRITING: Writing informal emails

1 Read the email. Then number the sentences 1–5.

Hi Geeta,

How are you? I hope the family are all well.

I wanted to tell you about my trip to Ramsgate with my friends from class on Saturday. It was fantastic! We started early and travelled by train. We arrived at ten o'clock. First, we visited a museum and listened to an interesting tour guide talk about the history of Ramsgate. Then we ate fish and chips in an old pub. After that, we walked around Ramsgate, but we were tired so we stopped on the beach and had ice cream. It was a traditional day at the English seaside!

Please tell me your news. Did you do anything special at the weekend?

Take care,

Mishiko

a They sat next to the sea. _____
b They arrived in Ramsgate. _____
c They learned about the town's past. _____
d They looked at the town. _____
e They had lunch. _____

2 Choose the correct options to complete 1–7.

1_____ James,

How are 2_____?
I hope 3_____ are well.

Did I 4_____ you about my holiday? We went to Marrakech in Morocco. It's an amazing place! Here's a photo of me in the local market.

Take 5_____ and 6_____ you soon!

Bye for 7_____,

Tracey

	a	b	c
1	Bye	See	Hi
2	well	things	they
3	things	you	it
4	tell	ask	want
5	soon	care	well
6	see	are	hope
7	well	you	now

3 Number the pictures 1–3. Then complete the sentences.

a _____
b _____
c _____

1 Nora got home at half past seven.
   First, _____.
   Then _____.
   After that, _____.

a _____
b _____
c _____

2 Gavin had a very busy day.
   First, _____.
   Then _____.
   After that, _____.

4 Reply to Mishiko's email. Tell her what you did last weekend. Make sure you

• start and end your email in a friendly way.
• use sequencers to show the order of events.

HOME   BLOG   PODCASTS   ABOUT   CONTACT

Learning Curve

Tom and Sam talk about watching live events.

LISTENING

1 ▶ 7.5 Listen to the podcast about live events. Tick (✔) the correct box for each person.

	Live	TV
Speaker 1 prefers		
Speaker 2 prefers		
Speaker 3 prefers		
Speaker 4 prefers		
Tom prefers		
Sam prefers		

2 ▶ 7.5 Listen again. Complete the sentences with one word from the podcast.

1 The survey said that _____ people prefer live events to TV.
2 Speaker 1 _____ watches football on TV.
3 He likes singing songs with his _____.
4 The weather at the _____ festival wasn't good.
5 Speaker 2 and her friends danced for _____.
6 Speaker 3 says the _____ was boring.
7 She can see the _____ better on TV.
8 Speaker 4 likes looking at _____ in art galleries.
9 He went to a gallery a few _____ ago.
10 Sam says that Tom is _____ because he prefers TV to live events.

READING

1 Read Simon's blog about celebrities. Match the celebrities with photos a–d.

1 Hugh Jackman   _____
2 Lady Gaga   _____
3 Kanye West   _____
4 Jennifer Hudson _____

2 Read the blog again. Write T (true), F (false), or NG (not given) if there is no information in the blog.

1 Hugh Jackman was in eight *X-Men* films.   _____
2 He lived in England for twelve months.   _____
3 Lady Gaga helps other people.   _____
4 She worked as a waitress to pay for school.   _____
5 Kanye West didn't like working in the shop.   _____
6 His parents paid for all his clothes.   _____
7 His company's clothes are expensive.   _____
8 *Dreamgirls* is a film about a restaurant.   _____
9 Jennifer Hudson was born in Chicago.   _____
10 She never eats burgers.   _____

3 Order the letters to make celebrity jobs.

1 limf tiredroc   _____ _____
2 carnig ridrev   _____ _____
3 flatrobole   _____ _____
4 healtet   _____ _____
5 noishaf dolem   _____ _____
6 netsin reyalp   _____ _____
7 terriw   _____ _____
8 sminciua   _____ _____

HOME **BLOG** PODCASTS ABOUT CONTACT

Our guest blogger Simon tells us what some stars of music and film did in the past.

Before they were STARS

Most celebrities spend their days doing really cool and exciting things. But their lives weren't always so interesting. In fact some celebrities had very normal jobs before they were famous.

In 2000 **Hugh Jackman** played the part of Wolverine in X-Men. The movie was very successful and he was the star of eight more X-Movies in the noughties and the twenty-tens. But Hugh had other jobs before he was an actor. When he was only eighteen he moved to England from Australia. He was a teacher in a very expensive school. His students liked him very much but after a year he moved back to Australia.

These days everyone knows **Lady Gaga** for her music, her amazing shows and her interesting clothes. She sells millions of records and she works for a lot of charities. On the 11th December 2015, people chose her as the 'Woman of the Year 2015'. But before she was famous, when she was at school, she worked as a waitress near her home in New York. She says she wanted the money to buy an expensive bag!

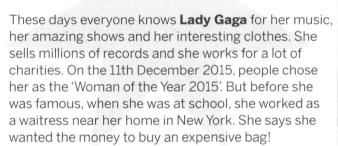

When **Kanye West** was a teenager he worked in a clothes shop. He liked the clothes but he didn't enjoy the job. And he didn't make much money. In fact, he didn't earn enough money to buy the clothes in the shop! Today he is one of the most famous musicians in the world and makes millions and millions of dollars. And in 2015 his company started selling clothes. And they aren't cheap!

Jennifer Hudson is a very famous actress and singer. She was the star of the film Dreamgirls in 2006. But her first job was at a Burger King restaurant in Chicago, USA. She started work in the restaurant when she was sixteen. Everyone says she liked to sing a lot at work! In 2007, Burger King called Jennifer to say she never needs to pay for food – she gets free food for life!

Travel

GRAMMAR: Past simple: irregular verbs

1 Write the past simple verbs.

1 We h_____ a loud noise from the street.

2 Karen s_____ her money on clothes.

3 Noone k_____ the answer to her question.

4 Who t_____ you English last year?

5 Brendan f_____ a wallet on the bus.

6 Sue w_____ a letter to her grandmother.

7 They b_____ some vegetables at the market.

8 He c_____ a new lamp for his study.

2 Complete the sentences with the past simple verbs.

Across

1 This shirt only _____ me €20 at the shopping centre.

3 She _____ her house keys in her bag.

5 I _____ my boyfriend at university in 2016.

6 They _____ to Cartagena in an old car.

7 He _____ me a call on my mobile last night.

8 It _____ three days to paint our new house.

Down

1 Who _____ first in yesterday's race?

2 Her cat _____ next to her on the sofa.

4 I _____ about singing at the party but I'm a horrible singer so I didn't!

6 We _____ the housework then went to bed early.

VOCABULARY: Travel verbs

3 Choose one option in each sentence which is <u>not</u> correct.

1 He *got in / got on / took* a taxi to the station.

2 Do you know how to ride a *bike / horse / car*?

3 I don't want to miss my *bike / bus / train* tomorrow!

4 Let's take *a taxi / a bus / a car* to the hospital.

5 They *flew / got off / got in* from London to France.

6 We can book our *flight / tickets / underground* on the internet.

7 Where do we *book / get off / ride* the train?

8 They *got off / got on / got lost* the bus at the supermarket.

4 Complete the sentences with travel verbs.

1 _____ the car, please. We need to leave now!

2 Can I _____ the flight online now, or do I need my passport?

3 I _____ the train to work. It gives me time to read and relax.

4 If you _____ the bus you need to wait for the next one.

5 Is it OK if we _____ to the park? It's a lovely evening and I don't have a bike.

6 You don't want to _____ so take a good map.

7 Most people prefer to _____ long distances because planes are fast.

8 She can't _____ her motorbike to work this week because her brother has it.

9 The ferry doesn't _____ when there is bad weather.

10 To go to the museum, take the tube and _____ at the third station.

PRONUNCIATION: Irregular past simple verbs

5 ▶8.1 Choose the correct sound for the verbs in each sentence. Then listen, check and repeat.

1 Bob got on the train at 6 a.m.	/ɒ/	/ɔː/	/əʊ/
2 Do you know he rode home?	/ɒ/	/ɔː/	/əʊ/
3 He walked to town and saw his friends.	/ɒ/	/ɔː/	/əʊ/
4 I thought I saw a tour guide.	/ɒ/	/ɔː/	/əʊ/
5 She drove to Rome.	/ɒ/	/ɔː/	/əʊ/
6 Paul lost his ticket.	/ɒ/	/ɔː/	/əʊ/
7 They chose a cheap hotel.	/ɒ/	/ɔː/	/əʊ/

READING: Understanding the main idea

1 Write the words for weather and seasons.

1 It's w_____ and c_____ today.

2 It's s_____ in Germany.

3 In Edinburgh it's r_____ now.

4 In the mornings it's often f_____ but by lunchtime it's nearly always s_____.

5 A_____ and s_____ are good seasons to visit southern Europe.

6 When it's s_____ in North America, it's w_____ in South America.

2 Look at the title and the photos. Read the first sentences of each paragraph. Which question does the article answer?

a Why do we travel to places with warm weather?

b Why do people go to places with bad weather?

c Which countries have hot, cold and windy weather?

3 Read the whole article and choose the correct options.

1 The Marathon des Sables runners run in
   a hot weather b cold weather c hot and cold weather.

2 Mauro Prosperi got lost because
   a it was very hot b the weather was bad
   c he didn't have any water.

3 Scott's team went to Cape Crozier because
   a they wanted to be the first people there.
   b their friends were there.
   c they wanted to find something.

4 During the Antarctic journey the men didn't see
   a the sun. b many penguins. c any other people.

5 Windsurfers at the Défi races
   a come from many different countries.
   b sometimes travel at 144 kilometres an hour.
   c are all French.

6 The windsurfing speed record was in
   a France. b Namibia. c Gruissan.

4 Complete the sentences with *really*, *not very* or *quite*.

1 It is _____ foggy today – I can see the top of those hills.

2 Don't drink that coffee! It's _____ hot! Wait a few minutes.

3 I don't want to read the rest of this book. It's _____ good.

4 I'm _____ surprised you are here. I thought you were in Brazil.

5 It was _____ cold this morning. I needed a jumper when I wasn't in the sun.

6 That wasn't a good horror film last night. I was _____ scared at all!

7 Our exam was _____ easy. Some questions were difficult but I'm sure I passed.

8 You got three pizzas for only €12? That's _____ cheap!

Enjoying the **weather?**

Usually, when we travel, we go to places where the weather is warm and sunny. We don't like it when it's very hot, cold, windy or foggy. But some people look for extreme weather. Are they crazy? You decide!

A The Marathon des Sables is a six-day, 200-kilometre trek through the Sahara desert in southern Morocco. Runners carry everything they need with them, including water. It can reach 50°C, but at night they often sleep in temperatures below 0°! In 1994, Italian athlete Mauro Prosperi got lost for nine days after a sand storm. He ran 299 km in the wrong direction ... into Algeria!

B In July 1911, three members of Scott's team to the Antarctic travelled to a place called Cape Crozier. The men walked for 19 days in the 24-hour darkness of the Antarctic winter. They carried their food and tent behind them. It was sometimes –70°C. Why? They went to collect penguin eggs!

C Every year, more than a thousand windsurfers from 40 countries go to Gruissan in southern France for the Défi Wind races. This is an excellent place for windsurfing because it's very windy, with winds sometimes reaching 144 kilometres an hour. But Antoine Albeau holds the windsurfing speed record. He was in Namibia when he travelled at 98 kilometres an hour on November 2nd 2015.

GRAMMAR: *there was/were*

1 Match the two parts of the sentences.

1 At the party, there was some _____
2 There was a _____
3 There wasn't _____
4 There were _____
5 There were lots _____
6 There weren't _____
7 Was there _____
8 Were there _____

a a photographer? Yes, there was!
b a singer.
c any celebrities? No, there weren't.
d any waiters or waitresses.
e DJ all evening.
f of friendly people.
g great music.
h some sandwiches and cakes.

2 Complete the dialogue with *there was/were* in the correct form.

Pablo	Grandfather, ¹_____ any shops here in 1950?
Grandfather	Oh, yes, ²_____ lots of shops, but ³_____ only one shopping centre, and it was small.
Pablo	And what about places to eat?
Grandfather	Well, ⁴_____ some cafés, but ⁵_____ any pizza restaurants or places like that.
Pablo	⁶_____ a swimming pool?
Grandfather	No, ⁷_____. But ⁸_____ a park if you wanted to go for a walk.
Pablo	And what about transport? ⁹_____ a train station?
Grandfather	Yes, ¹⁰_____. It was very important, because ¹¹_____ many cars in those days.
Pablo	And what did you do in the evenings?
Grandfather	Well, ¹²_____ a nightclub for young people like there is today.
Pablo	That sounds boring!

VOCABULARY: Nature

3 ▶8.2 Complete each sentence with the words in the box. Then decide which picture each sentence describes. Listen and check.

grass	river	sea	sky	sun	tree

1 You can see it's windy today. Look at the _____!   a   b
2 There's a beautiful _____ above the water.   a   b
3 The evening _____ is very clear today.   a   b
4 The _____ next to the water looks very soft.   a   b
5 I don't think the water goes very fast along this _____.   a   b
6 You can still see the _____, but not for much longer.   a   b

4 Complete the nature words.

1 I can see a large black c___ ___ ___ ___ in the sky.
2 My dog loves to play in the f___ ___ ___ ___ next to our house.
3 Those f___ ___ ___ ___ ___ ___ are all different colours: red, yellow, and pink.
4 It's summer but it isn't hot up here on the m___ ___ ___ ___ ___ ___ ___ ___.
5 We had lunch on the b___ ___ ___ ___ but it was quite hot.
6 There are more than twenty types of tree in this f___ ___ ___ ___ ___.

PRONUNCIATION: Sentence stress

5 ▶8.3 Underline the stressed words. Then listen, check and repeat.

1 'Was there a television in your room?' 'No, there wasn't.'
2 'Was there an evening meal?' 'Yes, there was.'
3 'Were there any nightclubs?' 'Yes, there were.'
4 'Were there good restaurants?' 'No, there weren't.'
5 'Was there any music?' 'Yes, there was.'
6 'Were there many nice people?' 'No, there weren't!'
7 'Were there any shops?' 'Yes, there were.'
8 'Was there a swimming pool?' 'No, there wasn't.'

SPEAKING: Buying a ticket

1 ▶ 8.4 Listen to two telephone conversations. Find one mistake in A and one mistake in B and write the correct information.

1 Conversation 1: _____

2 Conversation 2: _____

A

FROM — Los Angeles
TO — Sao Paulo ✈

DEPART
15:05 13 November

ARRIVE
07:05 1 December

FLIGHT
LAK 0348

TICKET TYPE
One way

TOTAL (including airport tax):
$867.00 USD

B

BUS TICKET 🚌

RETURN

DEPART: **LONDON, Victoria Bus Station**

TIME **08:45** DATE **3 April**

ARRIVE: **GLASGOW, Central Bus Station**

TIME **16:50** DATE **3 April**

PRICE: **£73.50**

BUS NO: **4397** SEAT **6A**

BUS TICKET 🚌

RETURN

DEPART: **GLASGOW, Central Bus Station**

TIME **10:50** DATE **6 April**

ARRIVE: **LONDON, Victoria Bus Station**

TIME **20:30** DATE **6 April**

PRICE: **£73.50**

BUS NO: **4398** SEAT **10B**

2 ▶ 8.4 Listen again. Number the phrases 1–8 in the order you hear them.

a I'd like a ticket to Glasgow, please. _____

b When do you want to travel? _____

c Would you like a single or return ticket? _____

d What time does the flight leave? _____

e How much is it? _____

f I'd like a one-way ticket to Brazil, please. _____

g When does it arrive? _____

h What kind of ticket would you like? _____

3 ▶ 8.5 Order the words to make sentences and questions. Then listen and check.

1 a / Brisbane / I'd / like / return / ticket / to

_____.

2 does / it / time / leave / what

_____?

3 arrive / does / in / London / it / when

_____?

4 a / like / you / single / or / return / ticket / would

_____?

5 £8.90 / a / for / it's / single | ticket

_____.

6 do / return / to / want / when / you

_____?

4 ▶ 8.6 Listen and complete the conversations.

1 A _____, FPQ Couriers. _____
_____ Hanif speaking. How can I help you?

B Good _____. I'd like to speak to Mr Travers, please.

A Who's calling?

B _____ _____ _____ Diane Godridge.

~

C Thanks for _____, Miss Godridge. Goodbye.

B _____.

2 A Good _____. Jessica _____.

B Hello. _____ _____ William Sharp from Oldham Print Services. Is Karen there, please?

~

C Thanks for _____ _____, William.

B Thank you, Karen. _____ for now.

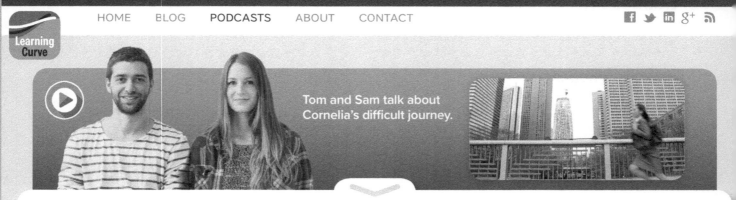

HOME   BLOG   **PODCASTS**   ABOUT   CONTACT

Tom and Sam talk about
Cornelia's difficult journey.

LISTENING

1 ▶ 8.7 Listen to the podcast about a bad journey. Number the things that happened (a–h) in the correct order (1–8).

a Cornelia took a taxi.   _____
b She asked a woman for help.   _____
c She used the internet.   _____
d She went to a café.   _____
e She ran very fast.   _____
f She got an email.   _____
g She fell over.   _____
h She asked a man for help.   _____

2 ▶ 8.7 Listen again. Choose the correct answers.

1 Cornelia got _____ about the interview.
   a a letter   b an email   c a phone call
2 Cornelia's interview was _____ miles from her home.
   a 300   b 200   c 100
3 She didn't fly because there weren't any _____ flights.
   a early   b cheap   c quick
4 She didn't know the _____ of her interview.
   a time   b address   c date
5 She took a _____ home from the station.
   a bus   b train   c taxi
6 The train was very _____.
   a fast   b expensive   c slow
7 At the station she asked a _____ for directions.
   a man   b woman   c tourist
8 There were only _____ minutes before the interview.
   a five   b fifteen   c 50
9 Cornelia had her interview in _____.
   a an office   b a shop   c a café
10 Cornelia didn't get _____.
   a the job   b a coffee   c an interview

READING

1 Read Marc's blog about South Korea. Match paragraphs 1–4 with photos a–d.

1 _____
2 _____
3 _____
4 _____

2 Read the blog again. Write Y (yes), N (no), or DS (doesn't say) if there is no information in the blog.

1 Marc thinks Korea is horrible in the summer.   _____
2 A lot of people go to Imjado beach.   _____
3 The weather in autumn is always warm.   _____
4 Marc thinks autumn is the best time to visit Seoul forest.   _____
5 It snows a lot all over South Korea.   _____
6 There are many mountains in Korea.   _____
7 You can't ski near Seoul.   _____
8 Spring is everyone's favourite season in South Korea.   _____
9 Marc doesn't like cherry blossom.   _____
10 Koreans often travel along the river by bike.   _____

HOME BLOG PODCASTS ABOUT CONTACT

This week's guest blogger Marc tells us why his parents' home country is a great place to visit at all times of the year.

SOUTH KOREA
a country for all seasons!

1 Summer (June to August)

When I was young, people always said to me, 'Don't come to Korea in summer – it's horrible!' It's true that it is very hot, but this is a good reason to go to the beach! The most famous beach is Haeundae near the city of Busan. It is very popular in the summer, with thousands of people enjoying the sun. In fact, sometimes it isn't very nice because of all the people. So try the island of Imjado for its quiet beach and beautiful sea.

2 Autumn (September to November)

The weather in autumn starts quite warm, but by the end of the season it's cold. If you are in the capital city, I recommend a visit to the Seoul Forest. It's a very big park in the centre of the city with more than 400,000 trees. Autumn is the perfect time to visit because the leaves on the trees are all different colours. It's beautiful!

3 Winter (December to February)

South Korea in winter is very cold and windy and it snows a lot in the north of the country, but there are still fun things to do. Remember that it has a lot of mountains so it's easy to find a place to ski. The best places to ski are in the east of the country, but that isn't the only place. You can even go on a skiing day-trip from Seoul. Then, go to a concert or music festival in the evening. There is lots of live music in Seoul.

4 Spring (March to May)

After the cold (and sometimes difficult) winter, the people are always happy at the start of spring. It often seems like everybody is out looking at the new flowers! South Korea is famous for its cherry blossoms – I think they are the most beautiful flowers in the world! When they're not looking at flowers, people often spend spring days cycling along the Han river. It's a long river with large areas of grass on either side. It's a very good way to get some sun on your face!

UNIT 9 Shopping

9A LANGUAGE

GRAMMAR: Present continuous

1 Choose the correct options to complete the sentences.

1 What's Viktoria *made* / *makes* / *making* in the kitchen at the moment?

2 Inzhu and Rayana *are* / *do* / *is* helping their brother with his new phone.

3 'Are you reading to Emily?' 'Yes, I *am* / *do* / *reading*. It's her favourite book.'

4 I'm not *use* / *uses* / *using* my bike this week.

5 Concepción and I *aren't* / *don't* / *isn't* talking to each other these days.

6 *Am* / *Are* / *Is* you and your friends getting ready to go out right now?

7 'Are Luka and Ibrahim playing basketball?' 'No they *aren't* / *don't* / *isn't*. It's netball.'

8 Aleksandre *am* / *aren't* / *isn't* working in the study today.

9 Rebecca's *watched* / *watches* / *watching* the football with her friends at the moment.

10 'Are we going to the supermarket? 'Yes, we *am* / *are* / *go*.'

2 Complete the sentences with the correct form of the verbs in brackets.

1 A What _____ right now? (do)
 B I'm on the bus. _____ to school. (go)

2 A _____ at a hotel at the moment? (stay)
 B No, we _____. We're in our tent. It's cold!

3 A I can hear another person with you. Who _____ to? (talk)
 B That's my grandmother. _____ her today. (visit)

4 A _____ in the competition? (swim)
 B Yes, they _____. They're in the pool right now.

5 A _____ dad _____ lunch ready? (get)
 B No, he _____ biscuits. I love his cooking! (make)

6 A What _____ in the bathroom? (do)
 B She _____ a shower. (have)

7 A _____ to Rome today? (drive)
 B Yes, but we _____ at a restaurant now. The driver needs to rest. (stop)

8 A _____ anyone _____ here at the moment? (sit)
 B No, that seat's free. And I _____ now, so you can have both seats! (leave)

VOCABULARY: Clothes

3 Complete the clothes words.

1 I like these s_____ and s_____ – they look good for my big feet!

2 It's snowing. Put a c_____ and h_____ on!

3 She wore a long red d_____ and a pair of beautiful brown b_____.

4 This j_____ keeps me warm in winter.

5 These t_____ are very big. I need a b_____ to make them stay up.

6 At weekends, I wear my old pair of blue j_____ and T-_____ with my favourite bands on them.

4 Look at the pictures and complete the crossword.

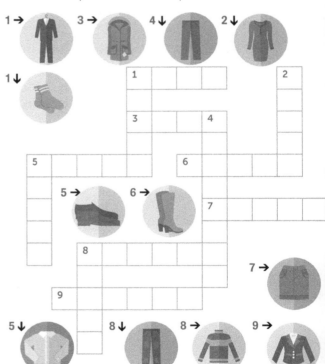

PRONUNCIATION: *-ing* endings

5 ▶9.1 Listen and repeat. Pay attention to the /ŋ/ sound.

1 Why are you going out?

2 Who's helping me do the housework?

3 I'm staying on my own.

4 I think she's speaking in Swahili.

5 We're just arriving now.

6 They're not looking after the house very well.

LISTENING: Identifying key points

1 ▶9.2 Listen to the podcast about the meanings of colours. Match the colours with the feelings.

1	in love	_____	a	black
2	angry	_____ _____	b	blue
3	calm	_____ _____ _____	c	green
4	sad	_____ _____ _____	d	red
5	scared	_____	e	white
			f	yellow

2 ▶9.2 Read these sentences from the podcast. Match them with a–d. Listen again and check.

1 So once again, colours change their meaning in different countries. _____   a emphasizing
2 Red hearts and red flowers show people that you love them. _____   b repeating
3 The reason for this is that when we are angry our faces are red. _____   c giving examples
4 Not just different – totally different! _____   d giving more information

3 ▶9.3 Listen to six sentences. Write the filler word (*er*, *so*, *um* or *well*) that you hear.

1 _____   4 _____
2 _____   5 _____
3 _____   6 _____

4 Complete the conversations with the correct adjectives.

1 angry / surprised

A Please don't be _____. I used all your milk.
I'm sorry.
B I'm just _____. You don't drink milk!

2 excited / worried

A Are you _____ about starting a new school?
B Yes, I am, but I'm _____ too. I hope the other students aren't unfriendly!

3 thirsty / hungry

A Are you feeling _____? Do you want a sandwich?
B No, but I am a bit _____. Can I have some juice?

4 calm / scared

A My sister is _____ by films like *Dracula* and *Frankenstein*.
B They certainly don't make me feel _____!

5 happy / tired

A Your brother doesn't look _____. Is he OK?
B He's fine, but he's quite _____. It was a long day at work.

6 bored / sad

A I'm not _____ that I didn't stay at the party. It was noisy and the food looked horrible.
B You did the right thing. I stayed and I was really _____!

GRAMMAR: *How often* + expressions of frequency

1 Number the frequency expressions 1–10, from the least often to the most often.

a   every month _____
b   every week _____
c   every year _____
d   four times a year _____
e   never _____1_____
f   once a day _____
g   twice a day _____
h   twice a week _____
i   twice a year _____
j   two or three times a month _____

2 Order the words to make sentences and questions.

1   **A** does / her family / how / Lupita / often / visit
_____?

   B a / goes / she / twice / usually / year
_____.

2   **A** does / every / exercise / he / week
_____?

   B a / goes / the gym / he / month / once / to
_____.

3   **A** a / a / haircut / have / I / twice / year
_____.

   B not / often / that's / very
_____!

4   **A** do / how / their parents / see / often / they
_____?

   B times / three / month / them / they / a / visit
_____.

5   **A** check / day / do / your emails / every / you
_____?

   B a / day / four / I / check / or / three / times
_____.

6   **A** always / does / go out / on / Saturdays / she
_____?

   B a / goes / month / once / or / she / out / twice
_____.

VOCABULARY: Shopping

3 ▶9.4 Number the sentences 1–9 in the correct order to make a paragraph. Then listen and check.

a   I usually shop at the market. It's friendly, but you have to pay with ... _____1_____
b   ... card at the shopping ... _____
c   ... cash there. You can pay by ... _____
d   ... centre. For presents I sometimes go to the department ... _____
e   ... my money at local ... _____
f   ... on. I want to start selling things online soon! _____
g   ... online for books and clothes, but not for shoes – you can't try them ... _____
h   ... shops. A few years ago I started shopping ... _____
i   ... store, but it's expensive. I prefer to spend ... _____

4 Complete the shopping words.

1   Do you want to g_____ s_____? Let's go now, before the s_____ c_____ closes.
2   At the m_____ you can b_____ meat, fish, fruit and vegetables.
3   This is a d_____ s_____, so why can't I p_____ b_____ card?
4   It's easy to s_____ lots of m_____ with just one click when you shop o_____.
5   She makes clothes and she s_____ them in a few of the l_____ s_____ in her town.
6   If you know your size, sometimes you don't need to t_____ o_____ new clothes.
7   You can only pay w_____ c_____ here. We don't have a card machine.

PRONUNCIATION: Sentence stress

5 ▶9.5 Underline the stressed words. Then listen, check and repeat.

1   He goes swimming twice a week.
2   They watch films two or three times a month.
3   I finish a book about once a week.
4   We have a holiday in Thailand every year.
5   Do you drive every day?
6   She has a shower once or twice a day.

WRITING: Describing a photo

1 Look at the photo and read the email. Find three differences between them.

> ● ● ●
>
> Hi Chloe,
>
> How are things? I hope you're well.
>
> I had a great time in London last weekend. I went with four of my friends from college. We took the bus and got there early. First we went to the Transport Museum, then we went shopping.
>
> Here's a photo of us in the street. We're carrying a lot of shopping! There are only three people in the photo because Karol is taking the photo. That's me on the left. Look! I'm wearing the black hat you bought for me. The boy at the top in a T-shirt is David. Paula and Alex are standing next to me.
>
> Email me soon, please. I want to know how the concert was.
>
> Izzie

2 Find one mistake in each sentence and write the correct words.

1 There are a shop window on the right of the photo. _____
2 They are four people in the photo. _____
3 They look in a shop window. _____
4 David is standing to the top. _____
5 The man in the left is Alex. _____
6 The other woman on the middle is Paula. _____

3 Look at the picture and write sentences.

1 That / our mother / middle

_____

2 My little sister Sofia / top

_____

3 She / sit / on my Dad

_____

4 David / middle, next / Mum

_____

5 There / Blackmoor Forest / top

_____

6 And that's me / right

_____

4 Choose a photo of you with your family or friends. Write an email to a friend and describe it. Make sure you

- explain who the people are and their position in the photo.
- use the present continuous to say what they are doing.
- use *there is/are* to say what things are in the photo.

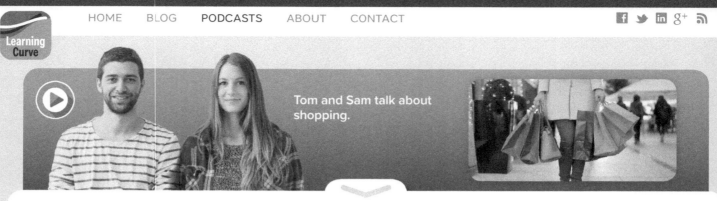

HOME   BLOG   PODCASTS   ABOUT   CONTACT

Tom and Sam talk about shopping.

LISTENING

1 ▶ 9.6 Listen to the podcast about clothes and shopping. Number the clothes 1–10 in the order you hear them.

a boots _____
b coat _____
c dress _____
d hat _____
e jeans _____
f jumper _____
g shirt _____
h shoes _____
i skirt _____
j trousers _____

2 ▶ 9.6 Listen to the podcast about clothes and shopping. How often do the speakers go shopping? Complete the sentences.

1 Speaker 1: every _____
2 Speaker 2: _____ times a week
3 Speaker 3: three times a _____
4 Speaker 4: every _____

3 ▶ 9.6 Listen again. Complete the sentences with one or two words.

1 Tom often wears the same _____.
2 Yesterday, Sam and Tom went to Greenway _____.
3 Speaker 1 is buying a _____ and _____.
4 Speaker 1 is paying by _____.
5 Speaker 2 is trying on _____.
6 Speaker 2 always shops _____.
7 Speaker 3 thinks the _____ is horrible.
8 Speaker 3 is meeting her _____.
9 Speaker 4 thinks the _____ has too many colours.
10 Speaker 4 thinks the _____ is beautiful.

READING

1 Read Simon's blog about emojis. Choose the best summary.

a Emojis are giving everyone problems.
b Everyone loves emojis because they are quick.
c Most people like emojis but Simon doesn't like them.

2 Read the blog again. Choose the correct answers to complete the sentences.

1 Simon's friends _____ send him emojis.
a sometimes
b often
c never

2 He says people _____ a new language with emojis.
a can learn
b don't need to learn
c are speaking

3 He didn't send his sister a message because he was _____.
a busy
b surprised
c angry

4 The message from his friend made him _____.
a worried
b bored
c sad

5 His girlfriend was angry because he didn't _____.
a use the right emoji
b reply to her message
c feel excited

6 He doesn't like emojis because _____.
a they're boring
b there are too many
c they can cause problems

HOME   **BLOG**   PODCASTS   ABOUT   CONTACT

Guest blogger Simon writes about the little pictures we send on our phones.

Em😳ji problems 😣

I hate emojis

There – I said it! My friends send me funny pictures every day but I don't like them. Do you want to know why? OK, but first let's look at why emojis are so popular.

First, they are quick. We live in a fast, busy world and it only takes a second to send an emoji. Next, they are international. British people, Brazilian people, Chinese people – we can all send and understand messages. And we don't need to learn a new language! And finally, a lot of people think emojis are fun. They make people laugh!

But emojis aren't always good. In fact, they often give me problems. Here are three stories from my life to show you what I mean!

Last year my sister had an interview for a very good job. She sent me this message: 'I got the job!' I was busy and I didn't have time to send her a message. So I sent a 'surprised' emoji. She replied with an 'angry' emoji. I didn't understand so I called her later. She asked why I sent her a 'surprised' face. 'You think I'm not good enough for the job!' she said. But it wasn't true!

An old friend sent me a message with some sad news. I tried to send a 'sad' face emoji to him but I was tired and I didn't have my glasses. And I sent him a 'bored' face! The next morning I saw my message and I was really worried! I called my friend and said sorry, but everything was OK.

My girlfriend and I went on holiday last year. The night before we flew, she sent me a message. It was a plane, a heart and a happy face. I tried to reply with an 'excited' face but I did it wrong. I sent her a 'scared' face. She didn't reply!

So that is why I don't like emojis. But sometimes I think everyone else loves them! Here are some interesting emoji facts. Did you know ...

- the first emoji was in 1999. A Japanese man called Shigetaka Kurita made it.

- July 17th is World Emoji Day. They chose that date because it is the date you can see on the emoji of a calendar.

- the world sends more than five billion emojis every day.

- the most popular emoji last year was the crying and laughing face. Second was the kissing emoji. And third was the red heart.

GRAMMAR: Present continuous for future plans

1 Order the words to complete the conversation.

A ¹ this weekend / you / doing / what / are?

B ² my grandfather / am / looking after / I. What about you? ³ you / tomorrow / are / studying?

A ⁴ I / am / yes. ⁵ going out / are / on Sunday / you? ⁶ practising for / we / our concert / are.

B That sounds great!

A ⁷ there / after lunch / is / Patricia / driving. Do you and Tom want to come with us?

B Yes, please. ⁸ in the morning / going / we / swimming / are. You can meet us at the pool!

1 _____?
2 _____.
3 _____?
4 _____.
5 _____?
6 _____.
7 _____.
8 _____.

2 Complete the sentences with the correct pairs of verbs in the present continuous.

write/enjoy	do/go	fly/see	help/cook
meet/take	not sail/drive	run/plan	visit/have

1 I _____ to Brazil on Monday but I _____ my grandparents there until Friday.

2 We _____ friends tomorrow morning. We _____ lunch at a restaurant together.

3 _____ you _____ anything tonight? Francine and I _____ to the cinema.

4 My sister _____ in the race next month. She _____ to run every day before then!

5 They _____ to Greece tomorrow on their boat. They _____ there instead.

6 _____ Harry _____ his mother at the airport this evening or _____ she _____ the bus?

7 When _____ he _____ his next book? I _____ this one very much.

8 I _____ Izzie to buy a new tablet tomorrow, then she _____ dinner for me.

VOCABULARY: Free-time activities

3 Choose one option in each sentence which is <u>not</u> correct.

1 Are they having a *video / barbecue / good time*?

2 I'm not staying in a *home / tent / hotel*.

3 Please can we visit *the museum / my parents / a hotel*?

4 Can I watch *a video / the football match / museum*?

5 We had the *art gallery / barbecue / party* in our garden.

6 Let's go to a *festival / a video / the beach*!

4 What are the people going to do? Complete the sentences.

1 I'm ready to relax in front of the TV. I'm w*atching* ___ *a* ___ *film* ___.

2 Malachi loves history and old objects. He is going to the city centre. He's v_____ _____ _____.

3 My parents are seeing their favourite musician. They're g_____ _____ _____ _____.

4 Parminder is tired after work. She wants a bath and an early night. She's s_____ _____ _____.

5 He enjoys looking at paintings and photographs. He is v_____ _____ _____ _____.

6 We're cooking in the garden today. We're h_____ _____ _____.

7 Alice enjoys being outside and seeing her favourite bands. This weekend she's g_____ _____ _____ _____.

PRONUNCIATION: Sentence stress

5 ▶10.1 Listen and repeat. Underline the stressed words.

1 A Who is she seeing tonight?
  B She's meeting her friends from university.

2 A Are they watching a film?
  B No, they aren't. They're watching the football.

3 A I'm visiting a friend in Dublin.
  B Are you taking the bus?

4 A Is he staying at home this evening?
  B Yes, he is. He's doing the housework.

5 A Which beach are you going to?
  B We're talking about that now.

6 A How are we getting there?
  B We're taking the train.

READING: Scanning for information

1 Quickly read the guide. Match events 1–7 with A–E. There are two extra events.

1 a film _____
2 a jazz concert _____
3 a classical concert _____
4 a rock concert _____
5 a festival _____
6 a talk _____
7 an art exhibition _____

2 Underline the key words in each question. Then scan the text for the answers.

1 How many bands are playing on Friday? _____
2 Which event is only in the morning? _____
3 How many events are only free for students? _____
4 How old do you need to be to watch the film? _____
5 What type of film is at the cinema this weekend? _____
6 How much is the art exhibition if you aren't a student? _____
7 What time does the event at Cambalache start? _____
8 Which two places are in the same road? _____ _____

3 Complete each sentence with the positive or negative imperative of the verbs in the box. There are two extra verbs.

be	book	buy	close	come
go	have	tell	wait	watch

1 _____ a ticket for me at the station. I already have one.
2 Please _____ to the next lesson with your questions about the film.
3 I'm working late tonight so _____ for me for dinner.
4 Tickets are expensive at the station so _____ them online the day before.
5 See you after the party. And _____ a good time!
6 _____ the door. I like it open.
7 I'm putting my coat on now. _____ without me!
8 _____ him I have a present for him. It's a secret.

THIS WEEK'S main events in and around town

A

Battle of the bands FINAL

See the best rock music in town. Three local bands are playing to win the £500 prize – don't miss it!
Friday 16th, 8 p.m.
Castle Arms pub, Crichton Street
£12, Students £10

B

Music of the 20s, 30s and 40s

A look back at the jazz of New Orleans. With Charles Rayburn and Lolo Gonzalez and his band.
Cambalache bar, Fenton Road, Saturday 10 p.m. till late!
£15

C

Variplex cinema

Police Force 2 - Action comedy
The second in the Police Force series – the first was exciting and funny!
**** The Daily Show, ****Movietime website
4.30 and 7.30 Sat and Sun
Tickets: £8.50 (+12 years) from cinema box office

D

Talk: 'From Dinosaur to Dodo'

Natural Science Museum
Wednesday 10.30–11.30 a.m.
Speakers include Margaret Pearson 'TV's dinosaur expert'. Come with questions!
Book online before Wednesday for free. School groups welcome! Find out more at www.NatSciMus.ed.uk

E

Fenton gallery

'Down' is an exhibition of landscape paintings and sculptures by local artists. Starts this week for two weeks only.
Monday to Friday 10–6, Fenton Road, admission £3 (free for students)

4 Order the letters to make words about music and films. Then write them in the correct category.

coinat	callsasic	mycoed	adarm	leecorntic	phi-pho
rorrho	zjaz	opp	cork	caronem	sceenic-oftinic

types of film	types of music
action _____	_____
_____	_____
_____	_____

GRAMMAR: Question review

1 Order the words to make questions.

1 a museum / did / last visit / when / Fabien

_____?

2 did / the concert / like / he

_____?

3 do / go / how often / to / the cinema / you

_____?

4 at the moment / can / bands / I / see / what

_____?

5 the festival / was / where

_____?

6 are / favourite / actors / who / your

_____?

7 DVD / it / can / on / watch / we

_____?

8 any / are / making / new films / soon / they

_____?

2 Match a–f with the questions in exercise 1.

a present simple _____

b present simple of *be* _____

c past simple _____ _____

d past simple of *be* _____

e present continuous _____

f with *can* _____ _____

3 Complete the questions with the verbs in brackets in the correct tense.

1 _____ you _____ a good book at the moment? (read)

2 What type of games _____ she _____ playing when she was a child? (like)

3 Who _____ your favourite writer now? (be)

4 How often _____ you usually _____ each year? (fly)

5 How many people _____ at his last party? (be)

6 _____ lots of supermarkets in your town these days? (be)

7 '_____ he _____ a musical instrument?' 'No, he can't.' (play)

8 When _____ you _____ shopping, next Saturday or Sunday? (go)

9 _____ Jean sometimes _____ to jazz music? (listen)

10 _____ you _____ that horror film last night? (see)

VOCABULARY: Sports and games

4 Choose the correct options to complete the sentences.

1 How often do you _____ running on the beach?
a play   b do   c go

2 I _____ gymnastics when I was a young girl.
a did   b played   c went

3 I told him I'm no good at chess but he still wanted to _____ with me.
a go   b do   c play

4 He _____ yoga at weekends.
a does   b goes   c plays

5 Last weekend they _____ rock climbing.
a played   b went   c did

6 She didn't study much at university. She mostly _____ video games!
a did   b played   c went

7 They're _____ football in the park.
a going   b doing   c playing

8 We're _____ skiing soon. I'm so excited!
a doing   b playing   c going

5 Complete the sports or games words.

1 Does he play h_____ on grass or ice?

2 I did k_____ until I got my blue belt; only the best people get a black one!

3 Is a r_____ the same as in American football?

4 Last winter we went s_____ in the Atlantic sea. It was really cold!

5 Most professional b_____ players are more than two metres tall.

6 I'm doing P_____. It's a bit like yoga.

7 One popular sport people play on the beach is v_____.

8 This weekend they're going w_____ in the hills while the weather is good.

9 Let's play t_____ tomorrow – with two more people we can play doubles.

10 He couldn't go c_____ yesterday because his bike is broken.

PRONUNCIATION: Intonation in questions

6 ▶10.2 Listen and repeat the questions. Pay attention to the intonation.

1 What's your hobby?

2 Are you doing it this weekend?

3 When did you start?

4 Was it difficult?

5 How often do you do it?

6 Is it expensive?

SPEAKING: Asking about a tourist attraction

1 ▶ 10.3 Listen to the conversation. Number the photos in the order the people talk about these things (1–5).

a _____   b _____   c _____   d _____   e _____

2 ▶ 10.3 Listen again. Are the sentences true (T) or false (F)?

1 The tourist knows Valparaiso well. _____
2 She and her boyfriend are staying in a hotel. _____
3 She wants to go in the Pablo Neruda museum. _____
4 The museum doesn't have a gift shop. _____
5 They want to go to the museum today. _____
6 On Saturday there is an event at the museum. _____
7 Her boyfriend needs to pay 2,500 pesos to get in. _____

3 ▶ 10.3 Read the sentences from the conversation. Which words did you hear? Listen again and check.

1 Is there a *café / gift shop*?
2 *When / Which days* is it open?
3 What time does it *close / open* today?
4 How do you *get there / pay*?
5 Are there any *concerts / special events* today?
6 What is there to do *if it rains / in the evening*?

4 ▶ 10.4 Listen to a conversation. Tick (✓) the expressions you hear. Who shows more interest, Graham or Tara?

1 Did you enjoy your trip? _____
2 How was your trip? _____
3 Did you have fun? _____
4 Oh, OK. _____
5 Oh really? _____
6 Sounds fantastic! _____
7 Sounds wonderful! _____
8 That sounds interesting. _____
9 What's that like? _____
10 Where did you go again? _____

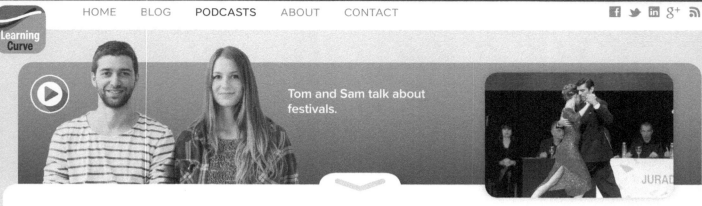

HOME   BLOG   **PODCASTS**   ABOUT   CONTACT

Learning Curve

Tom and Sam talk about festivals.

JURAD

LISTENING

1 ▶ 10.5 Listen to the podcast about festivals. Complete the table for the five festivals Anna is going to.

	Country	Type of festival
1	China	_____
2	_____	Comedy and _____
3	_____	_____
4	_____	_____
5	_____	_____

2 ▶ 10.5 Listen again. Write T (true), F (false), or NG (not given) if there is no information in the podcast.

1 Sam is going on holiday with university friends for the first time. _____

2 Anna always goes to festivals in the summer. _____

3 The Shanghai film festival only shows Chinese films. _____

4 Anna is driving to Edinburgh. _____

5 The Edinburgh Fringe festival is a month long. _____

6 Anna's parents live in Edinburgh. _____

7 You can't buy anything at the Santa Fe festival. _____

8 Anna is meeting a British friend in Santa Fe. _____

9 Anna is dancing in a competition. _____

10 Anna likes Indian music. _____

READING

1 Read Kate's blog about keeping fit. Match the photos with three of the paragraphs (1–6).

2 Read the blog again. Complete gaps 1–6 with questions a–f.

a I can't move very well in the morning. What is the problem?

b My brother says playing videogames gets us fit. Is this true?

c Why do people want to get fit? It's so boring!

d You ran a marathon last year. What did you do when you finished? And are you running any more marathons next year?

e I can't sleep at night and I often get ill. What can I do?

f I went running for the first time yesterday. Why are my knees hurting today?

3 Order the letters to make sports and games.

1 e a t r a k _____

2 t a b e l l _____

3 b u r g y _____

4 s h e s c _____

5 c o r k   g l i m c n i b _____

6 g i n s i k _____

7 n a s t y g i c s m _____

8 g l y c i n c _____

9 l a t e b l a b s k _____

10 l a n k w i g _____

HOME   **BLOG**   PODCASTS   ABOUT   CONTACT

Our guest blogger and 'fitness fanatic' Kate answers your questions about getting fit and keeping fit.

Questions for a 'fitness fanatic'

a

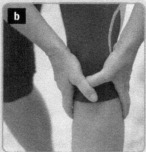
b

c

1 _____

I was so hungry after the race. I ate a big plate of rice and a special drink. It's really important to eat a lot after a lot of exercise. But before I ate, I lay down with my legs up in the air – it feels silly but it really helps! As for the future, I'm running the London marathon next year – wish me luck!

2 _____

I'm sorry to hear that. Were you running on grass or on the pavement? Running on hard ground can be really bad for the knees. Try running at the gym. It's less interesting, but it's better for your knees!

3 _____

What type of games is he playing? Because with some games you need to get up and move around. There are dancing games, for example, and games where you pretend you're playing tennis. These games can help you get fit. But it's much better to actually go dancing or play tennis!

4 _____

I have two words for you – go swimming! Did you know that swimming every day helps you sleep, makes you happy, and even helps you live longer? And swimmers get ill less than other people. So what are you waiting for? Jump in!

5 _____

Oh dear! My father had the same problem for years. Now he does pilates and yoga every week and he's like a child again. He jumps out of bed in the morning!

6 _____

There are so many reasons! Some people want to feel good and look good. Other people think exercise is relaxing and it makes them happy. Do you know the saying 'Healthy body, healthy mind'? Getting fit can help you think, study and work. And of course it's a great way to meet people!

WRITING: Writing informal emails

1 Read Sunan's email. Then match sentences a–g with gaps 1–6. There is one extra sentence.

a After that I went to bed.

b Bye for now!

c First, we visited an old castle near Sligo.

d Hi Kristof

e I hope you're well.

f I wanted to tell you about my holiday in Ireland.

g Then I took the bus to the west of Ireland.

To: Kristof Jansson

Subject: Ireland

Attachment: carla.jpg

1 _____ ,

2 _____ How was your summer?

3 _____ I was excited about taking the ferry to Dublin, but the weather was bad and it was two days before I travelled. So I didn't have much time in Ireland. But Ireland was beautiful and it was sunny when I was there.

First I visited Dublin – it's a fantastic city! 4_____. Carla, a friend, lives in a town called Sligo. She was happy for me to stay with her. But when I arrived at the bus station she wasn't there. She thought my visit was the next week, and she wasn't in town! I stayed in an expensive hotel that night. Sligo is small, and there wasn't much to do, so I went to a restaurant on my own. 5_____. How sad! ☹

But the rest of the holiday was great. Carla showed me some beautiful places (see photo).

6_____. See you next week.

Sunan

---

2 Complete the phrases with the words in the box.

about   care   hello   how   see   ask   things   well

Starting an email	Asking about the person	Saying why you are writing	Finishing the email
Hi Pete,	2 _____ are you?	Did I tell you	7 _____ you soon,
1 _____ Greta,	How are 3 _____?	5 _____ ...?	Bye for now,
	I hope you're 4 _____.	I wanted to 6 _____ you ...	Take 8 _____.

3 Complete the sentences with the correct sequencers, *after that*, *first* or *then*.

1 Juan was late for the exam. _____, there was a problem with the underground. _____ he missed the train. _____, he got lost when he tried to find the university.

2 _____, I found a recipe for chocolate cake on the internet. _____ I went to the shop to buy the things I needed. _____, I made the cake but I burned it!

3 Helena and Tara wanted to do something special. _____, they went to the park for a picnic, but it rained. _____ they decided to go to the cinema but there were no good films so they went home.

4 Carlos was tired after a long day at work. He had a coffee and _____ he went to the station but he fell asleep on the train. _____, he missed his stop and didn't get home until the next day!

4 Write an email to a friend. Tell them about a bad or difficult holiday or journey you went on.

- start and end your email in a friendly way
- ask about the person
- say why you are writing
- use sequencers to show the order of events.

WRITING: Describing a photo

1 Look at the photo and read Tiffany's email. Then choose the correct answers.

1 What did Ollie do last Saturday and Sunday?
   a He played games.
   b He went to a party.
   c He went to a festival.

2 Where was Tiffany at the same time?
   a at university
   b at a concert
   c in the country

3 What were they celebrating?
   a midsummer
   b Rut's birthday
   c the end of exams

4 What did they eat at the party?
   a cold food
   b a barbecue
   c nothing

5 How long was the party?
   a It finished at three o'clock.
   b It finished when it got dark.
   c It continued all night.

To: Oliver

Subject: Hello from Sweden!!!

Hi Ollie,

How are you? How was your weekend? Did you have fun at the festival?

I had a great time last weekend. We had a party at Loke and Rut's house in the country because it was the midsummer celebrations. In the day we had a barbecue, played games and swam in the lake. You can see lights at the top of the photo – we put them up because the party lasted all night. But it doesn't really get dark – we took this photo at 3.00 a.m!

Rut is the girl on the right. She's sitting in front of Loke. That's me at the top. I'm standing next to Peter. There are two boys playing guitar. They are Phil and Nikolas – they're excellent musicians! The girl on the left is Trudy, my friend from university. And the boy in the middle, sitting next to Phil, is Nils, Trudy's boyfriend. The other two are Rachel and Danilo, friends of Loke. We had such a good time!

See you soon,

Love Tiffany

2 Look at the photo and match the two parts of the sentences. Then complete a–g with the correct form of the verb *be*.

1 There	_c_	**a** _____ great night!	
2 Loke	____	**b** _____ a friend from university.	
3 Phil and Nikolas	____	**c** __*is*__ a beautiful red building behind us.	
4 Trudy	____	**d** _____ all listening to music.	
5 There	____	**e** _____ behind Rut.	
6 We	____	**f** _____ playing guitar.	
7 It	____	**g** _____ two people standing up.	

3 Look at the photo then complete the text with the words in the box.

in	bottom	left	middle	right	the	top

These are people I work with. The woman at the ¹_____ with short hair and grey trousers is my boss, Maribel. She's fun! The man on the ²_____ with the short black hair is David. He's the receptionist and he's very friendly. Then the older man on the ³_____ of the photo is Patrick. He's one of the engineers. Another engineer in my office is Gavin – he's behind Patrick. My best friend is Andrea – she is at the ⁴_____ of the photo with a book. And that's me ⁵_____ of Andrea and David. It's a great team!

4 Choose a photo of a party or celebration. Write an email to a friend and describe the photo.

   • explain who the people are in the photo.
   • use the present continuous to say what they are doing
   • use *there is/are* to say what things are in the photo.

58 St Aldates
Oxford
OX1 1ST
United Kingdom

Third reprint: 2023
ISBN: 978-84-668-2694-5
CP: 881104

© Richmond / Santillana Global S.L. 2018

Publishing Director: Deborah Tricker
Publisher: Simone Foster
Media Publisher: Sue Ashcroft
Workbook Publisher: Luke Baxter
Content Developer: David Cole-Powney
Editors: Sue Jones, Debra Emmett, Tom Hadland, Fiona Hunt, Laura Miranda, Helen Wendholt
Proofreaders: Pippa Mayfield, Shannon Niell, Jamie Bowman, Amanda Leigh
Design Manager: Lorna Heaslip
Cover Design: This Ain't Rock'n'Roll, London
Design & Layout: Lorna Heaslip, Dave Kuzmicki, emc design Ltd.
Photo Researcher: Magdalena Mayo
Learning Curve video: Mannic Media
Audio production: Tom, Dick and Debbie, TEFL Audio
App development: The Distance

We would also like to thank the following people for their valuable contribution to writing and developing the material:
Pamela Vittorio (Video Script Writer), Belen Fernandez (App Project Manager), Eleanor Clements (App Content Creator)

We would like to thank all those who have given their kind permission to reproduce material for this book:

Illustrators:
Simon Clare; Guillaume Gennet; Paul Dickinson c/o Lemonade; John Goodwin; Sean Longcroft c/o KJA Artists; The Boy Fitzhammond c/o NB Illustration Ltd.

Photos:
J. Escandell.com; J. Jaime; J. Lucas; S. Enríquez; 123RF; ALAMY/GerryRousseau, Jim Corwin, Moviestore collection Ltd, Simon Reddy, Stephen French, IanDagnall Computing, Joern Sackermann, dpa picture alliance, Serhii Kucher, ZUMA Press, Inc., All Canada Photos, London Entertainment, Everett Collection Inc, imageBROKER, Pongpun Ampawa, Peter Noyce GBR, Ian Allenden, AF archive, Elizabeth Livermore, Lex Rayton, Ted Foxx, Alvey & Towers Picture Library, Elizabeth Wake, Kristoffer Tripplaar, Lucas Vallecillos, Joe Fairs, Dinodia Photos, Peter D Noyce, Brigette Supernova, Pictorial Press Ltd, Collection Christophel, Jonathan Goldberg, Paul Hastie, Tierfotoagentur, REUTERS, Viktor Fischer, Art of Food, Andrey Armyagov, Alex Ramsay, Blend Images, B Christopher, Judith Collins, David Cabrera Navarro, Roman Tiraspolsky, robertharding, Michael Neelon(misc), Fredrik Kippe, Oleksiy Maksymenko Photography, Patti McConville, D. Callcut, Matthew Taylor, Rafael Angel Irusta Machin, Igor Kovalchuk, MallorcaImages, Paul Quayle, Jozef Polc, Mick Sinclair, Michael Willis, Hugh Threlfall, ITAR-TASS Photo Agency, Bailey-Cooper Photography, jeremy sutton-hibbert, creativeq, James Jeffrey Taylor, Oleksiy Maksymenko, Paul Smith, David Levenson, United Archives GmbH, Justin Kase zsixz, Simon Dack, Jeremy Pembrey, Barry Diomede, Alex Linch, Tomas Abad, Valentin Luggen, Sergey Soldatov, Iakov Filimonov, Anton Gvozdikov, Alex Segre, MBI, Paul Gibson, Stocksolutions, MEDIUM FORMAT COLLECTION/Balan Madhavan, allesalltag, David Robertson, Dmytro Zinkevych, Simon Dack News, Vaidas Bucys; CATERS NEWS AGENCY; FOCOLTONE; GETTY IMAGES SALES SPAIN/bjdlzx, Yuri_Arcurs, Reenya, Nikada, Paul Almasy, Martin Rose, Maskot, Lars Baron, JamieB, Annie Engel, Fosin2, Darumo, BraunS, artisticco, ajr_images, Bison_, AzmanL, artursfoto, pringletta, Dobino, Berezka_Klo, Indeed, Hero Images, KingWu, Tom Merton, NI QIN, Sam Edwards, Portra, ajaykampani, bgblue, leungchopan, c_kawi, s-c-s, kali9, SensorSpot, LeoPatrizi, Talaj, Pix11, Neyya, Dan Dalton, Chimpinski, DKart, shank_ali, Chris Ryan, londoneye, kickstand, kiankhoon, joto, Fuse, skynesher, asbe, gavran333, Zinkevych,